101 WAYS

TO
MEET YOUR
Angels

101 WAYS

TO MEET YOUR

Angels

Affirmations and Exercises to
Connect with and Learn from
Your Angelic Guardians

⮌ Karen Paolino Correia, CHT, ATP ⮌

Avon, Massachusetts

Published by
Adams Media, a division of F+W Media, Inc.
57 Littlefield Street, Avon, MA 02322. U.S.A.
www.adamsmedia.com

Contains material adapted and abridged from *The Everything® Guide to Angels*,
by Karen Paolino, CHT, ATP, copyright © 2009 by F+W Media, Inc.,
ISBN 10: 1-60550-121-2, ISBN 13: 978-1-60550-121-5.

ISBN 10: 1-4405-2981-7
ISBN 13: 978-1-4405-2981-8
eISBN 10: 1-4405-3037-8
eISBN 13: 978-1-4405-3037-1

Printed in the United States of America.

10   9   8   7   6   5   4   3   2   1

Library of Congress Cataloging-in-Publication Data
is available from the publisher.

This book is available at quantity discounts for bulk purchases.
For information, please call 1-800-289-0963.

CONTENTS

Introduction

Ask three people if they believe in the existence of angels, and what they think an angel is, and you will hear three different answers. Some people believe that when we die, if we have lived good lives in alignment with God's will, we will go to heaven to become angels ourselves. Others believe that God created the angels before humans and that angels are a superior race of spiritual beings, invisible to the human eye, and endowed with special powers. The word angel means "messenger," and they serve as God's messengers to bring divine guidance, provide protection, facilitate healing, and imprint the energy vibration of love on the hearts and minds of people in need.

Angel derives from the Greek word *aggelos*, also the Latin word *angelus*, meaning "messenger." Angels are spiritual beings who serve as intermediaries between God and humankind. They were created by the divine, just as humans were created, but angels are not the same as humans. In service of the divine, they perform many tasks as messengers, guardians, and helpers between heaven and earth. The more you open your awareness to discovering who they are and why they are here, the more you can invite miracles of love, support, and spiritual sustenance into your life. A belief in angels means you never have to feel alone or abandoned.

Angels make their presence known in many different ways, and if you detect an energy shift or strange scent, the likelihood of angel visitation is good. I hope you will use this book to discover other ways angels make their presence known, along with tips and strategies for summoning and working with these invisible helpers of God. These divine messengers are recognized by many of the great religious traditions of the world and they don't just descend from up high for major world events or for births and deaths. They are available to assist you in having a healthier, more joyful and abundant life right now. If you would like to call on your angels, work with them to improve your life, and develop a lifelong relationship with them, read on.

Part 1

BE PREPARED TO MEET THE ANGELS

The ancients described angels as spiritual beings created by God before the world was created. The tasks of these celestial beings are to glorify God, minister to the Divine, and serve as messengers, healers, and guides. Angels, in what is perhaps the most simplistic view, are akin to interpreters, passing messages between the divine and humans.

You might think a belief in angels is a matter of faith, and that is true. But it is also true that Judaism, Christianity, and Islam all share a belief in angels. Anecdotal evidence supporting that belief can be extrapolated from the ancient Hebrew texts, the early Christian writings in the New Testament, sacred verses of the Qur'an, and the written and oral esoteric teachings of Kabbalah (Jewish mysticism based on symbolic interpretation of their scriptures).

If you believe in angels, you are not alone. National polls prove it. According to a 2008 *Washington Times* poll, 55 percent of Americans believe in angels, while a *Fox News* poll from 2005 put the number at 79 percent. Additionally, a

2008 *ABC News* poll noted that 55 percent of Americans believe that their lives are protected by guardian angels.

But even national polls seem lightweight positioned alongside the mammoth amount of angel lore, references, and imagery prevalent in the world's cultures, religions, and spiritual traditions—a testament to ages-old belief in these celestial beings. Angel symbols and imagery have long permeated the world's art, literature, and musical lyrics, as well as pop culture's iconography. Both Harvard Divinity School and Boston College offer courses on angels, and books about angels such as *Angels in My Hair*, an international bestseller by Lorna Byrne and translated into twenty languages, and *Fallen*, by Lauren Kate have even made bestseller lists.

Perhaps you seek answers to your most burning questions, desire access to deeper spiritual truths, hope to contact a loved one who has passed on, seek a healing, or need protection. If so, consider following these ten tips as you embark on a special journey of contact with the angelic realm.

TEN STEPS TO PREPARE FOR YOUR MEETING

1. Read books; magazine and newspaper articles; blogs; and listen to/watch radio, television, and Internet broadcasts about angels, as well as follow the tweets of those who tweet about angels.
2. Keep an open mind about angelic forces around you.
3. Use periods of prayer, contemplation, meditation, and work through your dreams to make contact.
4. Try divination techniques, such as dousing, scrying, group meditations, and other modalities and methods, to access messages and information that may be obscured.
5. Maintain a journal of your efforts.
6. Form an angel support group to share ideas and experiences.
7. Take classes to learn more about angels from spiritual teachers in a variety of disciplines and traditions.
8. Pose questions for the angels and record responses.
9. Hone your instincts.
10. Be prepared to be amazed.

1: Cultivate an Open Mind

You don't have to be psychically gifted to connect or communicate with angels. As messengers from God, they are here to serve all of humanity. Just affirm your desire to know the angels, and open your heart and mind to receive their messages.

For this lifetime, you have been given two gifts: free will and free choice. Whatever choices you make and however those choices play out, the angels are watching with unconditional love. If you ask for assistance, they are at the ready. However, they will not interfere in your life unless you ask them, with one exception—if your life is threatened and it is not your time to die. In that situation, your tutelary or guardian angels will do whatever it takes to save your life, in a scenario known as divine intervention.

It is widely believed that each person has at least two guardian angels assigned to him or her by God, and those guardian angels remain near you from the moment of birth to the time of death. In addition to guardian angels, there are other divine helpers as well. The following three-tiered hierarchy lists ministering angels in God's divine order.

THE FIRST AND HIGHEST TIER

- **Seraphim** are the highest order of God's angelic servants and sit closest to the throne of God. These beings of pure light are so bright that humans have difficulty seeing them. Sometimes known as fiery serpents, they may appear with six wings and four heads. The seraphim choir or group includes Michael, Seraphiel, Jehoel, Kemuel, Metatron, Uriel, and Nathanael.

- **Cherubim** are the guardians of the fixed stars, keepers of the heavenly records, and bestowers of knowledge. Angels of harmony, protection, and wisdom, they channel positive energy from the divine. In Judeo-Christian theology, cherubim guarded the entrance to the garden of Eden against Adam and Eve after God banished them. The cherubim choir consists of Gabriel, Cherubiel, Ophaniel, Raphael, and Zophiel.
- **Thrones** bring God's justice to Earth. These celestial beings create and send positive energy to the Earth and its inhabitants. The throne choir includes Orifiel, Zaphkiel, Zabkiel, Jolhiel (or Zophiel), and Raziel.

THE SECOND TIER

- **Dominions** are the divine leaders who regulate the angels' duties. They are themselves angels of intuition and wisdom who manifest God's majesty. The dominion choir angels are Zadkiel, Hashmal, Zacharael, and Muriel.
- **Virtues** are the "the miracle angels," sent to Earth to help those who desire to make the impossible possible.

They bring harmony and peace into the world and assist those called to serve. The virtues choir angels include Uzziel, Gabriel, Michael, Peliel, Barbiel, Sabriel, Haniel, Hamaliel, and Tarshish.

- **Powers** defend and protect the world. They keep track of human history and are organizers of world religions. The powers choir includes Camael, Raphael, and Verchiel.

THE THIRD AND LOWEST TIER

- **Principalities** are the protectors of politics and religion, providing assistance to those dealing with leadership problems and human rights. In the Principalities choir are Nisroc, Naniel, Requel, Cerviel, and Amael.
- **Archangels** rule over all the angels and do not live in a reality of time and space. Therefore, they serve all of humanity—able to minister to an individual or the entire world simultaneously. They, too, interact with humans as messengers of the Divine. The archangels are Ariel, Azrael, Chamuel, Gabriel, Haniel, Jeremiel, Jophiel, Metatron, Michael, Raguel, Raphael, Raziel, Sandalphon, Ureil, and Zadkiel.
- **Angels** comprise the bottom rank of the hierarchy. Angels are the celestial beings working the closest with humans. There are many different kinds of angels in this

choir, including the guardian angels. The numbers are legion and their names too numerous and varied to list.

Ascended masters are not included in the angel hierarchy. But through special favor or dispensation of the Divine or having achieved enlightenment, these great teachers ascended into heaven and help those in need through miracles and healings. Among them are Blessed Mother Mary, Jesus, Quan Yin, Buddha, Moses, Mohammed, Serapis Bey, Saint Theresa, and Saint Francis. You may invite them into your life through prayers of veneration and supplication.

Finally, there are the fairies, also not mentioned in the angel hierarchy but nonetheless important because they are angels of nature. Becoming aware of the presence of the angels, fairies, and Ascended Masters requires setting aside skepticism, having an open mind, and desiring to see more than what physical eyes and senses may detect. Cultivating an open mind isn't difficult—you just have to be eager, ready, and willing to have communication with the angels, letting go of any bias or prejudice that might block the signs and signals of angelic presence.

2: Raise Your Vibration

Have you ever seen flashes or sparkles of light around you? Or have you witnessed the shadow of someone or something in your peripheral vision? Have you experienced synchronicity, strange sequencing of numbers, or unexplained coincidences? All can be manifestations of angel presence around you.

Tuning in to the vibration of angels means you may first have to raise your own vibration to detect and attune to higher and subtler levels of energy vibrations. Beckon the fairies and your guardian angels to aid in clearing your own energy field, and to help you tune in to their energy. Because the energy vibration of such spiritual beings is aligned with the earth, you will find fairies in fields, woodlands, and other natural settings. According to the human endeavor to qualify an angel hierarchy, fairies are between angels and humans.

Smile even if you are having a bad day, and notice how your energy changes. With a simple flexing of facial muscles into a smile, you have raised your vibration. Soon, you will be able to "sense" many different types of energy, even another person's life force. For example, someone who can sense higher vibrations will notice a faint energy or life force in the presence of someone who is ill or in a coma, versus a robust and vibrant energy force around a young, healthy person. Humans resonate energy between fear and love; angels vibrate the energy of pure love. To communicate with them, you will need to raise your vibration so that you can experience them with all of your senses.

The celestial vibration of angels becomes exceedingly important during a divine intervention. In such instances, angels can render assistance by superimposing their celestial energy upon another human being. The person chosen may be totally unaware that this is taking place and may act instinctively. So if you witness a person saving a life and being "in the right place at the right time," you may actually be witnessing an angel performing a miracle.

Refine your sensitivity to subtle energy by first tuning in to your own soul vibration. A great way to do this is through meditation on the energy centers, or chakras, of your etheric body, which is made of subtle energy in the likeness of your physical body. In the etheric body, seven chakras (a Sanskrit word meaning "wheels") ascend along the length of the spine from your tailbone to the crown of your head. By focusing your attention on these individual wheels or vortexes, you tune into the subtle vibrations of energy. The following exercises focus on the top four chakras.

CHAKRA MEDITATIONS TO RAISE YOUR VIBRATION

- Meditate on the *anahata* or heart chakra to see and merge your consciousness into the shining, effulgent light that is an aspect of the divine.
- Try some yoga breathing techniques (*pranayama*) to deepen meditation or raise your vibration (for example, practice rapid breathing for a short period followed by a period of quiet breathing).

- Meditate on the *vishuddha* chakra (at the throat center), where you use sound to communicate to the world. Meditate here to experience subtle sound vibration.
- Listen with attentive awareness to the ever-present cosmic vibration of the universe (AUM), and try to differentiate the subtle individual sounds within that current.
- Meditate on the *ajna* chakra (at the point between the eyebrows) to self-reflect and raise your conscious awareness of the subtle realms of the physical world.
- Breathe in and breathe out, saying your favorite name for God on the in breath and the counted number on the out breath.
- Meditate on the *sahasrara* chakra (located on the crown of your head), to connect your awareness to the pure and eternal divine consciousness.

Regular practice will raise your energy vibration closer to that of the angels and augment your communication efforts.

3: Expand Your Awareness of the Paranormal

The strong intuition of a psychic, the ability to hear extremely high-pitched sounds, and the ability to sense pain or heal through touch are examples of gifts that some people might call paranormal abilities. While some individuals are born with those talents, others develop them through the study of yoga, meditation, and other disciplines in order to increase their receptiveness and sensitivity to paranormal phenomena. Paranormal phenomena and events cannot be explained by science, and therefore remain mysterious, often relegated to realms of a spiritual or religious nature.

Similarly, the meaning of vibration from the *Merriam-Webster Dictionary* is "a characteristic emanation, aura, or spirit that infuses or vitalizes someone or something and that can be instinctively sensed or experienced." Meditation is one way to shift your vibration and expand your awareness of the paranormal. Meditation requires quieting of the mind and breath, for the two are intimately linked—when the breath slows, the mind becomes calm; conversely, when the breath is irregular or rapid, the thoughts in your mind jump around without focus or direction. In stillness, you find the gateway through which your consciousness, like a transmitter, can send messages and prayers or, like a receiver, accept divine inspiration, guidance, and love.

But you don't have to meditate to tune out the world. Think of your senses as devices clamoring for your attention. One by one you can turn them off (or down) and enter silence. In silence you can sense, feel, and experience the angels. Other ways to connect to the realms of the angels are through affirmations, chants, guided meditation, and prayers that you say using beads of a rosary or *japa mala*.

Choose to surround yourself with people who are positive, encouraging, and lift your mood and energy, rather than people who are negative, critical, fearful, angry, or prejudicial and who dampen your mood and drain your energy. Release your own fears, as fear lowers your energy vibration and blocks the flow of divine guidance. Fear reduces your ability to tune in to the higher vibrations of the paranormal world. Fear binds you to a lower vibration, fills you with dread and anxiety, and can immobilize your efforts to break free. Letting go of fear becomes easier if you affirm that God and the angels are watching over you during your every waking and sleeping moment. Saint Patrick of Ireland used to pray that the Lord was before him, beside him, behind him, beneath him, over him, in him and outside of him—therefore, what is there to fear?

4: Cultivate an Attitude of Appreciation and Gratitude

Everyone has a bag of troubles. It isn't the trouble we encounter or attract along the path of life, so much as the way that each of us deals with our troubles that raises or lowers our spiritual-energy vibration. Regardless of the daily challenges you may face, a conscious and loving relationship with your angels means you must immediately start to focus on the blessings already in your life, and feel appreciative for those. Practice recognizing the small things in life you are grateful for: a thank you or a smile from a stranger, a good cup of coffee, a sunny day, or time to read a good book.

To raise your vibration during difficult times, choose to focus on your blessings. If you are going through financial difficulties, be grateful for loose change in your pocket or items you can sell to pay for the essentials. Be grateful if you have a roof over your head and food to eat. If you are challenged with a physical illness, be grateful for the people who are willing to help you in your time of need. If you are grieving a loss of a loved one or your separation from a family member or friend, focus on the love and support from the individuals who are still in your life. When you focus on your blessings instead of your troubles, your vibration changes into a more positive, upbeat energy—the type that is more in tune with angel vibration. The following list includes a few more reasons to feel grateful.

- Your higher vibration becomes a powerful force for attracting good people, events, and things into your life.
- Angels want to work with you to help you experience heaven on earth.
- Gratitude fosters hope and the belief that the impossible can become possible.
- As you expand your awareness to the possibilities that exist, you increase your opportunities to experience myriad possibilities for yourself.

As you open yourself to the intangible world of the angels—a world that you can neither touch nor see with the human eye—you must expand your awareness, increase your intuitive abilities, and learn as much about angels as possible. Learn and be grateful for your ability to learn. Stretch your mind in the direction of new knowledge. Your desire and motivation creates the energy of enthusiasm that is like a magnet, drawing to you everything that you need to develop your skills. As you expand your knowledge and enhance your intuition, angels will have more ways to communicate with you. For example, if the angels see that you are paying attention to coincidences and synchronicities, then they will use this method of communication to get your attention.

5: Use the Power of Intention to Connect with Your Angels

Intention is a powerful and clear declaration of something you desire to attract into your life or a goal you want to reach. When you state an intention to the angels you set a powerful energy into motion. Your intention is an invisible force of energy that can make things happen. Get clear about what you want, and the rewards will be well worth the effort.

Remember, when working with the law of free will and free choice, you need to ask the angels for help. Write your intention of setting and following through with the goal of communicating with the angels. When you claim your intention and put it into action, you ignite the divine power within you to make things happen. Imagine what the results can be when you combine your power with the team of angels waiting to assist you. The possibilities are endless as you open yourself up to help, guidance, and clear communication with God and the angels. You can expect the manifestation of a miracle.

Here are some examples of stating intentions:

- Help me to release the fears that block clear communication with God and the angels.
- Heal my wounds from any past experiences that may block clear communication with God and the angels.
- Build my faith and trust, so I can believe in the existence of God and the angels.
- Help me to hear, see, and feel angelic presence around me.
- Help me to notice the ways in which the angels are trying to get my attention to answer my prayers.
- Show me the books and guide me to the people that will help me communicate with God and the angels.

The words and the method you choose to express each intention carry a different vibration of energy. Notice what the energy feels like when you hold an intention in thought. Then feel the energy increase when you write the thought down. Finally, feel the energy expand when you clearly enunciate the intention. The more energy you put into declaring your intention to your angels, the more powerful your intention becomes.

6: Be Skeptical but Open

If you are like most people, when you are alone and hear a door closing or footsteps on the stairs, or see a shadow flitting away from your peripheral vision, you will most likely seek a logical explanation for the event. But when logic and science fail to explain the phenomena, do you consider paranormal possibilities, including the presence of angels?

Skepticism has a place in the human psyche because it keeps people from a gullibility that could be to their detriment. But rigid skepticism renders a belief in angels near impossible. You must set aside your skepticism if you are to open your heart and mind to the help, guidance, and wisdom of angels in your life. After all, angels are nearly as old as time, with images of them predating even early Judaism. In fact, some scholars say that the earliest religious representation of angels dates back to the city of Ur, in the Euphrates Valley, from about 4000 to 2500 B.C. A *stele,* or stone slab, from that part of the world shows a winged figure descending from one of the seven heavens, to pour the water of life from an overflowing jar into a cup held by the king.

Other records show that in Mesopotamia, there were giant winged creatures that were part human and part animal, known as griffins. And in Egypt, Nephthys, the twin sister of the goddess Isis, is shown in paintings and reliefs enfolding the dead in her beautiful wings. Her image is found carved on the inner right-hand door of Shrine III in the tomb of Tutankhamen, circa fourteenth century B.C. Her angelic representation encompasses the dead pharaoh and protects him from all harm.

The ancient Egyptians believed that each person born into the world had a supernatural double, called a *ka*, which was born alongside them and stayed as a part of his or her life thereafter. The *ka* was what you might consider a guardian angel. Sometimes there is a simple or obvious explanation for events that seem a little out of the ordinary; but for those times when logic doesn't explain an event, set aside your skepticism and consider that paranormal phenomena might be at work.

7: Put Your Belief in Angels in Context

Angels were integral to the cultural, spiritual, and religious milieu of the ancient world, both before and after the birth of monotheism. In the Bible, some angels served as harbingers of death and destruction while others aided humans during times of great stress. Angels provided solace, announced news, brought good tidings, offered warnings, sang celestial hymns, and delivered God's wisdom to His people. The following traditional beliefs and stories about angels are included to provide a perspective of angel beliefs in a Judeo-Christian context.

ANGELS IN HEBREW SCRIPTURE

The Old Testament contains several stories about the ancient Hebrews' contact with angels. In some cases, angels revealed themselves; at other times, they remained unseen. Whether they provided protection, counsel, succor, or the means of redemption—according to the beliefs of the ancient Hebrews—they were fulfilling divine purpose. The stories about Hagar, Jacob, Abraham and Isaac, and Moses, and their contact with angels, remain important threads in the tapestry that began the Jewish story.

HAGAR AND ISHMAEL

Perhaps you have read the Bible, and will recall that in Genesis, the first book of the Old Testament, angels contacted the young Egyptian handmaiden Hagar. Hagar had become pregnant by Abraham, the Hebrew tribal leader. Abraham's wife Sarah was barren and Hagar's attitude, as the "second wife" to Abraham, troubled Sarah. When Hagar could take no more conflict with Sarah, Hagar fled into the desert. On the road to the city called Shur, she approached a spring. There, while Hagar rested, the angel of God told her to return home to bear her son and to call him Ishmael. Later, through God's grace, the aged Sarah bears Isaac, whom she sees as Abraham's true heir. The relationship between Sarah and Hagar again became so contentious that at Sarah's behest,

Abraham exiles Hagar and Ishmael to the desert. Lacking the protection of Abraham and the tribe, and dying of thirst with no spring or well in sight, Hagar put her child in the shade of a bush, begging God not to let her see her child's death. Then she wept and prayed. An angel of God called to Hagar from heaven asking, "What aileth, thee, Hagar? Fear not; for God has heard the voice of the lad where he is" (Genesis 21:16). The angel's purpose surely was to comfort and guide Hagar, for the scripture states, "God opened her eyes and she saw a well of water; and she went and filled the skin with water, and gave the lad a drink. And God was with the lad" (Genesis 21:19-20).

JACOB

Elsewhere in Genesis are accounts of angel encounters with Jacob, Abraham's grandson. Jacob had a shaded history of bad choices; he cheated his brother Esau out of his inheritance, he tricked his uncle Laban out of all his wealth and possessions, he married twice and he had illegitimate children. Later in his life Jacob feared death at the hands of Esau even as he desired forgiveness. One night, Jacob wrestled with an angel until dawn until Jacob finally won the struggle and demanded a boon (blessing). Jacob deduced that since he had emerged victorious over the supernatural being, all would be well with his brother; because the angel had understood Jacob's desire to make peace with Esau, it was. Jacob remained deeply involved with angelic presences all through his life.

Abraham and Isaac

One of the most famous biblical stories of angels is found in Genesis 22:11. The narrative features Hebrew patriarch Abraham, and his son Isaac. One day, Abraham heard the voice of God, spoken through an angel, calling out to him. The voice instructed the old man to sacrifice his beloved son Isaac. Abraham was to take the boy to a remote mountain and slit his throat in the manner of the usual sacrificial lamb and to let his blood run out as an offering, to prove to God that he would surrender to his will. The obedient Abraham took his son to the top of the mountain, laid him across an altar, and raised the knife to sacrifice his beloved son. Then an angel appeared. The angel commanded him to stop, "Lay not thy hand upon the lad." Abraham obeyed. At that moment, he spotted a sheep with its woolly fleece entangled in the thorns of a bush. He caught it and sacrificed it, offering it to God in place of his son Isaac.

Moses

A protective angel helped Moses, and the Jewish people, as they searched for the promised land after their forty-year enslavement by the Egyptian pharaoh. A biblical passage in the Book of Numbers reveals, "But when we cried out to the Lord, He heard our voice and sent an angel and brought us out of Egypt" (Numbers 20:16). The angel not only oversaw the exodus of the Israelites led by Moses, he also parted the waters of the Red Sea, making crossing possible. Then when the powerful Egyptian army approached, the "Angel of God" who had been moving ahead of the camp of Israel went behind it, creating a cloud that separated Moses and his people from the Egyptians pursuing them.

ANGELS IN THE NEW TESTAMENT

As religious beliefs transformed, so did people's views of the angels, as evidenced by angel imagery in the New Testament. Gone are the Old Testament angels, who performed heroic deeds and brought death, destruction, and vengeance. In the New Testament, angels are personified through power. They are no longer abstract extensions of God, devoid of personality, but rather "friends" to humans, to be called upon in times of stress or need. The archangels now possess names. They, and the other angels, serve important roles in the stories of Jesus' birth, crucifixion, entombment, and resurrection. As you read and reflect upon the following New Testament stories about angels, perhaps there will be one or more angels to whom you feel an attraction, and you'll desire to make a personal connection.

ANGELS OF ANNUNCIATION

The angel Gabriel appeared to the Virgin Mary to announce that she would bear the Son of God. This event, known as the Annunciation, is a central tenet of Christian belief. During the visitation, the angel told her not to be afraid, and explained that she had found favor with God. "And behold, thou shalt conceive in thy womb, and bring forth a son, and thou shalt call his name Jesus" (Luke 1:31). When Joseph, who was betrothed to Mary, felt embarrassed by her obvious pregnancy, an angel appeared to him in a dream saying, "Joseph, son of David, do not be afraid . . . for that which has been conceived in her is of the Holy Spirit. And she will bear a Son; and you shall call His name Jesus, for it is He who will save His people from their sins." After the birth of Jesus, the angel continued to look after the holy family and appeared twice to Joseph, giving him instructions on where to go to keep his family safe. Prior to his appearance before the Virgin Mary, Gabriel had also appeared to Zacharias, a priest who was married to Elizabeth, cousin of the Virgin Mary. The angel visited Zacharias when he was burning incense in a temple. Gabriel announced Elizabeth's pregnancy to her husband there. Since Zacharias did not believe the angel, the angel struck the priest mute until his son John, later to be known as John the Baptist, was born.

Angel Appearances after the Crucifixion of Christ

Angel sightings and visitations are important aspects of the stories belonging to the New Testament Apocrypha (sacred texts excluded from the Bible for various reasons, including disputed authenticity), such as *The Vision of Paul* and *The Ascension of Isaiah*. In the case of Paul, an angel guided him through various realms of heaven and hell, and about 3,000 angels sang a hymn before him as he approached the city of Christ. Later, Paul witnessed 200 singing angels preceding Mary, and after entering the gates of Paradise, she explained to him that he had been granted the unusual favor of coming to that place before he had finished his earthly life. After entering the gates of Paradise, Paul encounters the ancient prophet Enoch in the third heaven, who issues a warning to Paul not to reveal what he has seen. Then the angel descends with Paul to the second heaven, and thence to the earthly paradise, where the souls of those deemed righteous await the resurrection.

THE ANGEL AT JESUS' TOMB

The four Gospels of Matthew, Mark, Luke, and John include stories about the Resurrection, when Jesus rose from death. In Matthew, an angel sits on the stone that covered the mouth of His tomb, and Mary Magdalene and (the other) Mary see the angel when they arrive to anoint the body of Jesus (Matthew 28:2). Mark's gospel reveals two women, Mary Magdalene and Mary, the mother of James and Salome, arriving at the tomb with sweet spices to anoint the body of Jesus. Finding the stone rolled away, they entered and saw "a young man sitting on the right side, clothed in a long white garment" (Mark 16:5). The Gospel of Luke states that there were two men in shining garments who told the women Jesus had risen (Luke 24: 4-6). The Gospel of John notes that Mary Magdalene went to the tomb in the darkness before daybreak, saw that the stone covering the sepulcher had been taken away, and ran to fetch Peter and the other disciple whom Jesus loved (John 20:1-4). The two disciples ran to the tomb, looked inside, and saw nothing but the linen that had been used to wrap Jesus' body. The men returned home, leaving Mary Magdalene, who stayed at the tomb and wept. At last, peering inside, she saw two angels in white, "sitting, the one at the head, and the other at the feet, where the body of Jesus had lain" (John 20:12).

ANGEL WORSHIP POSED ISSUES FOR THE EARLY CHURCH

During the early Christian era, many people believed in and even worshipped the angels despite the apostle Paul's stance against angel worship. The presbyters and bishops of the early church believed a clear distinction had to be made between the angels and Christ. They taught that only God and His son were to be worshipped, Christ was the communicator closest to the Heavenly Father, and the angels served as lesser intermediaries between God and His people. The First Council of Nicaea in 325 A.D. proclaimed angel worship in keeping with other beliefs that the church held as true (dogma) but another council reversed that decision in 343 A.D. Finally the controversy ended in 787 A.D. when the second Council of Nicaea declared a limited dogma of the archangels which included their names, specific functions, and legitimacy of their images in art.

8: Invite Angels Into Your Home

Belief in angels can be inspired or enhanced by time spent in sacred spaces. Such areas do not have to conform to constructions for ritualistic purposes, but rather they can be places where holy beings of spiritual realms are always welcomed. Constantine the Great (306-377 A.D.), the first Christian emperor of the Roman Empire, declared that angels have wings. Subsequently, during and after his reign, angel imagery included winged angels in churches, cemeteries, and other sacred places. If you want to welcome angels into your home, garden, or workplace, angel imagery with or without wings can serve your purpose. Hang posters, framed art or calendars, or add angel statuary in a designated place. For example, allocate an area or room in your home, a corner of your cubicle or office, or a protected area of the garden where you can sit undisturbed to reflect and pray. If you prefer beckoning angels while in nature, choose a familiar gulley or a field, a favorite sitting area under a tree, or bank of a lake, river, or pond. Maybe you enjoy sitting amid sand dunes where you can watch blades of grass waving in the sea breeze. Or perhaps you prefer a special rock in a canyon, in the desert, or on a hillside. The point is to find a place that you feel safe, protected, sheltered, and comfortable. That place becomes holy by your presence, thoughts, affirmations, supplications, and prayers. Angel images inspire you to beckon the angels. When they come, welcome them with an open mind, a loving heart, and respect and gratitude for all they do.

Here are some suggestions for creating your sacred space:

- Play peaceful music.
- Display pictures of your favorite religious deities.
- Display pictures of your loved ones, living or deceased.
- Light candles to create the right energy.
- Arrange crystals or rocks collected from meaning places.
- Arrange pictures or statues of angels.
- Find a special journal in which to write.
- Put down a fountain with the soothing sound of water.
- Turn the ringer on your phone off.

After your sacred space is created, set your intention that this is your special place to come, where you can let go, pray, and be open to the gifts and miracles of angels. Each and every time you enter your space, invite the angels to gather and ask them to surround you in their loving light and protection. Ask them to fill your space with the highest vibration of divine white light and energy, and know that with every breath that you take you will become one with this sacred healing light.

Start your day by entering your sacred space, and ask the angels to fill your day with blessings. During the day, ask them to show you what you need to know. Enter the sacred space at night, and release fears and worries to the angels. Offer thanks, gratitude, and appreciation to the angels.

9: Incubate Angel Dreams

The ancient Egyptians practiced *dreaming true*, or using the dream state to ask and receive answers from the gods. The ancient Greeks engaged in *dream incubation*, usually near water such as springs, lakes, rivers, or the sea, invoking Asclepius, god of healing. You can practice a similar technique of dream incubation by taking a warm bath, and preparing yourself to beckon the angels to meet you in the dreamtime. The following checklist will help you to get started.

HOW TO INCUBATE DREAMS INVOLVING ANGELS

- Change your bed linens to make the sleep environment fresh and clean.
- Put a sachet bag of rosemary, lavender, or mint near your pillow.
- Keep the lighting soft with a candle or lamp.
- Take a warm, scented bath and dress in a clean gown or pajamas.
- Put a pencil and paper within easy reach.
- Ask your guardian angels to protect you while you sleep.
- Declare what you wish to see or learn in your dream, and invoke an angel by name, or call upon your guardian angels to meet you in the dreamtime.
- Extinguish the candle or lamp.

- Meditate on your question and ask for the answer as you slowly descend into sleep.
- Lie quietly upon waking and revisit your dream request, as you recall as many details of your dream as possible.
- Write down your dream, or fragments of it. If the meaning isn't readily clear, consult a dream dictionary for meanings of your dream symbols.

Regular practice of dream incubation techniques will help you more easily gain clarity about life issues or problems for which you seek answers. You will find the boundaries between waking and dreaming become blurred and as fragments of your dream enter your mind throughout the day, insights and even the answers you seek, will come.

10: Keep Detailed Notes of Your Experiences with Angels

Whenever you have contact with your angels, whether in the dreamtime, in meditation, or at any other time, jot down detailed notes to reinforce what you saw, heard, tasted, smelled, or felt. This diary of details will reinforce your thinking about angels, and it will also help you begin to distinguish which angels come to you, and the circumstances of their appearances. For example, do the angels come only when you invite them or have a question? Or do they visit you in your time of need? Do they visit when you are anticipating them and feeling peaceful? The following six suggestions are designed to help you log and write about angel visitations.

THINGS TO NOTICE AND RECORD ABOUT ANGEL VISITS

1. When, where, and how did it occur?
2. What were you doing, and what was your mood?
3. What exactly happened—write down all the detail you can recall.
4. Which of your senses detected the paranormal activity or angel presence? What did it feel like?
5. What did you do when you realized something was different? If the level of your curiosity or intensity of your feelings shifted, describe the difference before, during, and after.
6. How did the contact end?

If contact with the angels is a new experience for you, keep a journal to help you understand what might be the most effective way for you to detect the presence of angels. It is also helpful to know and recognize the different types of angels.

Part 2

KNOW THE DIFFERENT TYPES OF ANGELS

The hierarchic system of the angels is the result of human design, not that of the angels. Seraphim and cherubim were mentioned in the Old Testament, but then Dionysius the Areopagite, a disciple of Saint Paul, purportedly added seven more in the New Testament: thrones, dominions, virtues, powers, principalities, archangels, and angels.

Some modern religious scholars take issue with the idea of angelic hierarchies. One philosopher, Mortimer Adler, finds such speculation [of angel ranking] "highly entertaining." And Christian evangelist writer Timothy Jones, in *Celebration of Angels*, states that "However tantalizing the recorded glimpses of angels in Scripture are, they are ultimately just that: glimpses. We can take great comfort, however, in knowing that populating the heavenly spheres are creatures so great they boggle and frustrate our every attempt to pin them down."

Ranking the angels according to a hierarchy may indeed be the work of humans, but it is easy to understand why someone would create a system around which to sort all the information about angels that spans centuries, and ecclesiastical, as well as secular literature and art. A ranking system enables us to more easily assimilate the available information in order to understand the identities of these heavenly beings, their divine purposes, and importance to our lives.

11: Get to Know Your Guardian Angels

From birth to death, your guardian angels are ever near, shadowing your every move. Think of them as divine helpers, immediately available to respond to your summons. Their love for you is unconditional. Nothing you can say or do changes that. Your job is to accept that at your side throughout your life is a loving, helpful, albeit invisible companion. Your angels have names, and you can discover those names by beginning a dialogue, asking questions and receiving answers. Open a dialogue with your guardian angels just as you would with a new friend. For example, ask questions such as "What is your name?" "I would like a sign to know you are near; what sign shall we use?" Or, simply ask questions requiring a yes/no response such as, "Shall we meet each day at 3:00 P.M.?" By welcoming your angels, and taking time to pray with them, you draw ever closer to them, becoming more perceptive to cues in your environment, or to feelings that alert you to their nearness. As you establish a rapport with your angels, recognize their presence, and call them by name, you will begin an amazing journey that can only be described as transformational.

The benefits of maintaining a relationship with your guardian angels are many. They can help you find a life partner that is perfect for you, or aid you in developing a wider social network. In times of trouble, they can assuage your fear and worry, and guide you to solutions. Your guardian angels can make their presence known to deceptive people and otherwise protect you from harm, help you with your business, or aid in resolving any health problems.

12: Connect with Nature Angels

Spend time in nature if you wish to connect with fairies, for they are nature angels. Converse with them and express your desires, intentions, and requests. Ask the fairies to clear your energy and raise your vibration so you can attract only good into your life. Then listen and connect with their playful wisdom, and allow them to guide you. Since they are nature angels, they will team up with you even more if they see you picking up trash that others have left behind. They ask you to use products that are environmentally conscious and to do what you can to respect and safeguard the Earth. Just as you appreciate and need help from the angels, the fairies likely appreciate your loving care of Mother Earth.

Fairies are believed to be playful and creative, and for this reason children are more likely to see them and enjoy their presence. However, fairies also like to assist adults, and will nudge you to have more relaxation time to play, especially if your days are heavily scheduled with work and family responsibilities. Ask them to help you find a soul mate, and they will become matchmakers to help you find that perfect partner. They love creativity and will provide inspiration to help you with any project: designing your gardens, your home, or any other creative endeavor. The fairies can serve as powerful forces in helping you manifest your dreams. Ask them to gather around you, and give them a wish list of what you want and need. Then ask them to show you that the impossible is possible. Be open to their miracles of manifestation, and trust that they will joyfully help you. Then pay attention, and watch the magic unfold.

The following list suggests ways to meet the fairies and how to invite them into your life. As with the other angels, the nature angels, or fairies, have always been available to you. Now you are choosing to see and experience them. Pay attention to the gifts they bring into your life.

- Take your journal to the park and sit a spell enjoying nature. Invite the fairies to gather round and inspire you with ideas for a creative project, or help you solve a problem.
- Plant a flower garden and place statues of fairies in it. Make a sign that says, "Fairies welcome."
- Take a picnic lunch into a woodland area, and invite the fairies to join you for lunch. Bring along a recorder (a cell phone with voice notes functionality, a tape recorder, etc.) and, as if you were conversing with a friend, pose questions for the fairies. Then, as answers pop into your head, record them. Sit on a bench to watch children playing on a playground or in the park. Ask the fairies to bless you with a glimpse of them, and then watch for any signs of paranormal activity.

- Volunteer to pick up trash, help remove graffiti, or take part in some sort of outdoor charity work in your community. Invite the fairies to join you by mentally attuning to their vibration and asking them to keep you company as you enhance the beauty and health of your local environment.

13: Look to the Ascended Masters for Guidance

The ascended masters were once embodied as humans and faced the same challenges that you, and all other humans, face during your lifetimes. It is widely believed that the ascended masters, although they have achieved mastery over matter and their bodies are not physical, can manifest themselves in tangible human form if they so choose. It is also believed that they can manifest as streams of light. The prophet Isaiah explained how to reach and recognize the ascended masters, who are humankind's spiritual teachers. Over two millennia ago he observed, "And though the Lord give you the bread of adversity, and the water of affliction, yet shall not thy teachers be removed into a corner any more, but thine eyes shall see thy teachers; and thine eyes shall hear a word behind thee, saying, "This is the way, walk ye in it, when ye turn to the right hand, and when ye turn to the left" (Isaiah 30:20-21).

To reach the ascended masters, retire into a period of silence and meditate. They respond to feeling, thought, and intention. In quiet meditation, with your physical eyes closed and turned gently toward the point between your eyebrows, search to see a blue or white light, or star. Focus on it and mentally send forth a soul call to one of the ascended masters. Mother Mary, for example is a powerful ascended master of love, compassion, and wisdom. She provides protection for women and children, facilitates healing, and guides those who feel lost, confused, or abandoned. Mahavatar Babaji is known as the eternal yogi. Anecdotal evidence of the presence of this deathless avatar and master of the religion of Siddha Yoga is rare, but in one case he was perceived as light (like a star) moving from the evening sky into the physical form of a man. Maitreya, beloved of Buddhists as the "embodiment of loving-kindness," works to bring about the enlightenment of humankind. The ascended masters appear when you are ready, and when you desire to loosen the various fetters that bind you to this earthly incarnation in order to become a more evolved spiritual being. These teachers will provide you with the guidance and help you need. But it is up to you to call on them.

14: Reconnect with Your Loved Ones in Spirit

Many people believe that heaven is a far-off place, but heaven according to the twentieth-century saint and teacher Paramahansa Yogananda is nearer than you might think.

According to him it is just behind the gross vibration of the world of matter, or the world inhabited by humans. To contact the astral world or loved ones in heaven, you must refine your senses to become spiritually attuned to their vibration. When you refine your own senses to connect your energy to the more refined vibratory astral realms of spirit, it is possible to communicate with those who have passed on. It is you who decides whether, in the process of attempting communication with a loved one, to be the broadcasting unit or the receiving instrument. It takes intense concentration and a powerful desire to make that connection. Deeply attune your heart, mind, and spirit to God until you feel centered and grounded before sending your thoughts to your loved ones through the point between your eyebrows. To receive messages, put your attention in your heart center and focus on them there.

Spiritualists suggest that although the souls of those who have passed over exist in a body of spirit, aspects of their human personalities may still be apparent. For example, you seek advice from a relative, perhaps a favorite uncle in spirit, about buying a new home. You have tried contacting him. Every time you attempt to contact your uncle, you get an overwhelming the feeling that you should not waste your money. If that relative been fiscally conservative in life, insisting on saving money and always advising against spending it, that personality trait of your uncle might still be present in him and influencing the insights you receive.

15: Identify Fallen Angels

Avoid mindlessly meditating and inadvertently being open to lower vibrations which can feel like fearful apparitions or beings of a dark nature, such as earthbound spirits. Beings of a dark nature are not spirits willing to help you with your positive journey. Angels glow in the energy of pure light and love. They communicate only messages of love and encouragement. They always act and guide from a place of unconditional love. This is not so with fallen angels. You should know immediately if you're dealing with an angel or a fallen angel. Fallen angels are defined in Judaism, Christianity, and Islam, as angels who have been banished from heaven for rebelling against or disobeying the Divine. Lucifer, a fallen angel, emerged as synonymous with Satan in Christian belief during the fifth century. The Qur'an also mentions Satan as a Jinn, or mischievous, disobedient spirit, and associates Satan with other angels prior to his fall from grace.

In Revelation, the last book in the Bible's New Testament, Saint John the Divine, states, "And there was war in heaven: Michael and his angels fought against the dragon: and the dragon fought and his angels, And prevailed not; neither was their place found any more in heaven." (Revelation 12:7-8).

Earthbound spirits, or deceased humans who are hanging around the earth plane, are technically not fallen angels, but rather "ghosts." If you recognize these "earthbound spirits" through a perception of their dark energy, and you feel fearful, call upon Archangel Michael and ask him to escort them back home. Also ask the archangel to remove any fear or darkness. Shift your thoughts to focus on God's light and unconditional love for you. In no time you should feel safe, but if you still sense fear or agitation, continually call out to the angels to surround you in light.

16: Meet Angels of Birth and Death

Angels of birth help you transition into this life. Although it is unlikely that you would remember it, it is likely that this angel was present for your birth. Many people find it comforting to know that special angels are there for each birth, whether it is theirs or the birth of their children or grandchildren. Some people believe an "angel twin" or guardian angel accompanies each soul as it is born into this world; and others think that there are special angels who attend the birth to make sure that all is well, and then depart for other birthings. The author of *Angels in Action*, Robert H. Kirven, says, "spiritual protection of infants is typical of angelic occupations in that it is a kind of service [and that] angels have a special affection for newborn children." Kirven further explains that other angels and spirits replace these earliest guardians when infants grow out of infancy and into childhood. The question as to whether the *first* angel assigned to a child is the lifetime guardian angel has never been definitively answered.

Kirven bases his opinion on his extensive study of the works of the eighteenth-century scientist-turned-mystic Emanuel Swedenborg.

Angels also attend death. Emanuel Swedenborg, who wrote prolifically about angels, gives an account of how he first encountered "some of the kindest and most profoundly loving of all angels," in what we would today call a near-death experience. He explains that people "wake up" after dying, gradually becoming aware of angels positioned at their heads. These "death angels" are apparently able to communicate with persons who have just died and make them feel peaceful, safe, and happily welcomed to their new state of being. The transition period, whether it is easy for the person that has passed or difficult (for some resist believing they are dead), is supervised by these special angels.

Part 3

USE THE POWERS OF INTENTION AND COMMUNICATION TO ATTRACT YOUR ANGELS

Now that you have learned some tips for tuning up your vibration and some ways to connect with the different types of angels, you are ready to use your knowledge and skill to attract your angels whenever you want. Proper understanding of the power of thought will prove instrumental to your ability to work with the angels to manifest healing, abundance, loving relationships, and other things that you desire to have in your life.

Consider for a moment the possibility that everything in the universe is a massive force of thoughts. Imagine that all that has been, or will be created, had its beginning as a thought in the mind of the Creator. This thought force has unlimited potential. Use the power of intention enhanced by clear thoughts (your mind power), a laser focus, and the energy vibration of love and gratitude to begin to working with the angels, to shift various aspects of your life into more positive avenues. Through your mind power, which is a conscious yoking of your will to thoughts and feelings, it is possible to draw things you want, circumstances you seek, and relationships you desire with humans, as well as spiritual beings.

Believing in God and the angels requires patience. You want certain things to happen now, and sometimes it's just a matter of time. During these restless moments, pray for patience, keep the faith, and believe the angels are working behind the scenes. Ask the angels to empower you with patience and perseverance, and trust that your desire is coming to fruition.

17: Focus on Clarity: "Clear" Seeing, Hearing, Feeling, Knowing, Tasting, and Smelling

Make certain that you strive for clarity when you ask the angels to communicate with you.

Communication from the angels flows through your psychic senses, called "clair" senses. These correspond with the senses of seeing, feeling, hearing, knowing, tasting, and smelling. When any one or more of these clairs are taking in information, pay close attention to what is being sensed. When you do, you are better able to receive clear communication from God and the angels. The following list distinguishes between the different clairs.

- *Clairvoyance* is clear vision. This is when you have visions, images, or symbols presented to you through your "inner" vision.
- *Clairsentience* is clear feeling. This is when you receive information as a feeling in your body.
- *Clairaudience* is clear hearing. This is when you experience or hear clear thoughts or words flowing through your mind when no one is physically talking to you.
- *Claircognizance* is clear knowing. When you have an inner knowing, you feel very strong that something is true or you know beyond any doubt that you need to take action.

- *Clairgustance* is clear taste. When you experience this, you have a clear taste of something in your mouth without any explanation of why it's happening.
- *Clairolfactory* is clear smell. When you use this ability, you can smell something even though it's not physically in your presence.

Some people may be more sensitive to what they feel, or they are clairsentient; their intuition speaks to them through sensations in their body. Others may be more sensitive to what they hear (they are clairaudient), and their intuition is sparked by hearing something speaking to them through their inner thoughts or ideas. Seek to discover which senses you use the most and which ones seem to receive intuitive information the most clearly. The following eight questions serve to help you assess your intuition level. Answer yes or no. The more "yes" responses, the more likely it is that you are using your intuition.

1. Do you see signs of synchronicity and coincidences?
2. Do you notice fleeting movements of light or shadow?
3. Do you hear high pitches or sounds without an obvious source?
4. Ever feel a tingling sensation or feathers lightly touching your skin?
5. Do you smell otherworldly perfumes like floral or musky incense, again, without a source?
6. Do you sometimes taste nectar upon your tongue?

7. Or, do you ever feel the sensation of a hand, in yours or upon your shoulder, when you are alone?
8. Do you suddenly have special moments or epiphany after praying over some dilemma or issue?

You might find it helpful to create a mental toolbox in which to store and recall experiences with the angels. And, while we are on the subject of mental recall, another important point is worth mentioning.

As you walk your spiritual path and learn more about the angels, you may find that some of your previously held religious beliefs no longer fit you—there's a sense that you've grown beyond them in some way. What you learned as a child had its place, but your spiritual knowledge expands as you gain new information, insights, and experiences. What you once held as truth might not feel as true or even right. In fact, you may even be releasing some of your old religious beliefs. Trust and be patient with yourself if you are going through these changes.

The following list of action items includes things you can do to feel empowered as you shed old thinking and ideology for new.

- Write a short prayer to say when you feel weak in mind or spirit, or confused.
- Keep your journal handy with notes for quick reference about your angels and guides and how they can help you.

- Recite an affirmation such as, "I am God's creation and co-creator with the Divine. I therefore choose to surround myself with positive energy, light, and the love of the angels and God."
- Wear a rubber band around your arm, and flick it when you want to remind yourself that just because you cannot see something does not mean that it does not exist. This type of repeated action can be effective in helping you change thought patterns.
- Sing a song about angels or make up a chant that extols their loving energy or the importance of loving yourself as the angels love you.
- Ask the angels to walk the walk with you in the new direction you've chosen.

18: Overcome the Ego

The ego is the aspect of you that distinguishes your "self" from the selves of others. It is the "I" of you. To develop and train your intuition means you will, at times, be overriding or setting aside your ego to perceive and accept incoming psychic or intuitional information as true. Your ego might demand scientific proof of something that, your intuition tells you, is a paranormal intangible occurrence and cannot be measured or judged using scientific method. Overriding your ego means you will learn to trust that what you are hearing, feeling, and sensing is indeed from the angels.

You are more intuitive than you realize. The more you can understand and listen to your intuition, the better it can guide you. Below is a list of expressions that people use when they are connected to their intuition. Check to see if you use any of these phrases.

- *"I had a feeling."* Have you ever had a feeling that something was going to happen, and then it did? Did you ever have the feeling you needed to call someone, and when you did they needed your help?
- *"Something told me."* Did you ever hear an inner voice guide you, telling you what to do?
- *"I had a dream."* Did you ever get a direct message from someone in a dream, or did you ever have a dream that later had significant meaning?
- *"I had a gut feeling."* Did you ever not trust your gut feeling, and disaster followed? Now think about a time when you did follow your gut feeling, and everything worked out.
- *"I just knew."* Did you ever have that inner understanding where you knew you were right, and nobody could change your mind?

Learning to set aside an ego urge, in favor of taking in information through intuition, will pay big dividends as your intuitive powers increase along with more regular responses from the angels. Try not to discount what your senses tell you, even when the ego is asking you to do just that. Take the time to interpret the signs and messages you may be receiving from the angels.

EXERCISE TO DEVELOP YOUR INTUITION

- Close your eyes and place your hand on your heart.
- Take two slow, deep breaths.
- Ask which friend or family member needs to receive a phone call from you.
- Wait for a name to pop into your mind.
- Notice how you feel when you hear that name.
- Ask if there is anything further you need to know.
- Wait for the mental response.
- Call that person and see how accurate your intuition was.

Be aware that sometimes angels provide direct guidance, as if your intuitional messages were literal and true, with no interpretation needed. At other times, angel guidance can be symbolic. In those times, ask the angels to interpret and further guide you. Also, don't be afraid to ask the angels to always give you direct guidance instead of symbols.

19: Push Aside Fears to More Easily Connect with Your Angels

Overcome fear through transformative thinking in order to lighten your spirit, raise your energy vibration, and open yourself to angel visitation. Fear can close you off to paranormal experience. In the extreme, fear can cause you to clamp down and quit trying to have contact with the angels. You might not be able to completely banish fear (at least initially), but you can try to work through it with the help of your angels. Ask them for assistance. Seek their protection against negative thoughts or images that arise in your imagination. Request that they encircle you in a shield of protective light to dispel any negative energy forces that you sense around you.

Replace worries or dread and anxiety with thoughts that are hopeful, positive, and lighthearted. If you are a worrier, always fearing one thing or another, make it a goal to break the habit of fear. Meditate, and affirm your desire to replace the habit of feeling fearful and worrying with a habit of trust, belief, and faith in your own powers and the support of the angels. When you break that habit, you empower yourself. The following short technique might prove helpful.

- Sit for a period of meditation.
- Concentrate your attention at the point between the eyebrows (the center of will).

- Affirm that you are erasing the bad habit of worrying, as though it were a pencil line on a page of white paper.
- Call upon your angels to help you erase the bad habit, and replace it with the good habit of trusting that all your needs are being met and you are always being inspired with how to meet your daily life's needs.
- Feel hope, peace, and trust in the form of light fill your body and mind. Stay in the joyful place as long as you can, returning to it when fear creeps in again.

20: Invoke the Archangel Michael for Psychic Protection

While it may not always feel like it, you have the power to surround yourself with a protective safety net that blocks negative psychic energy, whether it comes from within you or from points outside of your physical body. You can always invoke the Archangel Michael, the "field commander" of God's army, for protection against such unwanted negative or dark forces. He will fill your mind with courage and strength, and you will soon feel the peaceful protection of the light and love of the divine helper.

In the Bible's Old Testament, an unnamed numinous being (that some believe was the Archangel Michael) appeared with sword in hand, prompting a man named Joshua to fall down with his face toward the earth, and to ask the angel what words he had brought from the Lord. "And the captain of the Lord's host said unto Joshua, Loose thy shoe from off thy foot; for the place whereon thou standest is holy. And Joshua did so" (Joshua 5:14-15).

In art, Michael is usually depicted as having wings and holding his sword while (often) standing upon the Devil or a slain dragon that represents Satan. In the Hebrew Apocrypha Book of Enoch, Michael is one of several archangels that always accompanies God the Father whenever He (Yahweh) departs from His throne. Michael has been associated with healing ever since he purportedly caused healing waters to flow from a spring in Colossae during the first century. Since that time, people seeking healing and protection have called upon Michael and flocked to churches honoring him. There have been sightings of apparitions resembling this angel since about the fifth century. If you see a numinous being with an unsheathed sword and feel a sense of victory or mercy, or feel restored to health and wholeness, you are likely being blessed by the presence of the archangel Michael.

Archangel Michael is the leader of the archangels. His name means "he who is like God," and he is the archangel of protection and the patron saint of policemen. His sword symbolizes his ability to cut through all fear and resistance. He lends his courage and his strength to anyone who calls on him. Michael has a fiery energy, and when you invoke him it's very possible you might feel warm or even begin to sweat. If you tap into your clairvoyance, you might see the colors purple and blue, which are associated with Archangel

Michael's presence. Call on Archangel Michael, and he will help you with protection of all kinds. He will empower you with the courage you need for any situation.

PRAYER FOR PROTECTION BY ARCHANGEL MICHAEL

Archangel Michael, please come to me now and surround me in your protective shield of light. Please clear my energy field and release me from all negativity. Help me to feel safe and protected in your loving presence, and provide me with the courage I need. Amen.

21: Breathe in the Wisdom of the Angels

You can use the wisdom of God and the angels in your life by inviting them to give you guidance. To invite divine guidance, do breath work to raise your vibration and to enhance your connection to the world of spirits. *Breath* is synonymous with *spirit*. Breath is your gateway to the sacred angelic dimension.

Life cannot exist without breath. As breath is involuntary, you are unaware of your breathing until you experience a shortness of breath or a speeding up of breath (hyperventilation) when you feel fear, stress, or panic. But you can use conscious and controlled slow breathing to connect your spiritual self to the sacred realm.

Engaging in breathwork, yoked with a gently focused consciousness, helps you contact the angelic realms and also refines and enhances your natural mental, physical, emotional, and spiritual abilities. Such work unblocks energy pathways and permits an inward flow of information into your consciousness. The breath is a powerful tool for raising your vibration so you can access sacred information from other dimensions. Conscious breathing develops a communication link between body and mind, between conscious and unconscious, and between spirit and angels. Try the following simple exercise to tie up the mind with the breath, to connect with your inner power, and to raise your energy vibration.

CONSCIOUS BREATHWORK EXERCISE

1. Relax and close your eyes. Observe your breath pattern, but do not make any attempt to alter it. Notice the breaths going in and out. Slow the breaths and breathe more deeply. Feel the warmth of the air as you exhale. Feel the cool new breaths as you inhale. Imagine your whole body being cleansed and energized by each breath cycle.

2. Listen to the sounds you make while breathing. Don't judge, just listen attentively. Notice whether

the breaths are shallow or deep. What moves when you breathe in, your diaphragm or belly?

3. Connect the inhaled breath with the exhaled breath, so that your breathing is one continuous movement. Continue doing this for several minutes and notice how you feel.

Breathwork can heighten your mental concentration. After doing breathwork, hold the image of numinous angels before your mind's eye, and call to them. Broadcast your desire for them to join you now that you have prepared a calm, serene mental state and a slower beating heart. Ask them to meet you in the temple of your heart. Sit quiet for some time just in awareness.

22: Invite Angels Into Your Life Using the Law of Attraction

The law of attraction is a New Age belief that like attracts like. So if you think negative thoughts, they bring more negativity into your life. If you embrace positive thoughts, you are attracting positive influences into your life. It is not wishful daydreaming. It is not fanciful thinking. Meditate about angels to attract their positive influence into your life. Study the different angels from Part 1 of this book, and consider how each angel makes you feel. Record these feelings in your journal. If one particular angel makes you feel safe and protected, you are inviting that energy into your life. When you feel in need of protection, revisit your journal and attract the feeling of protection into your life.

Some say this ancient law has been around since the beginning of time—or possibly at the beginning of human consciousness. Your thoughts never really stop. You can slow them. You can change the quality of them from negative to positive, but they are always freely associating; that is, you jump from one thought about a particular subject to another thought (maybe on the same subject, maybe different), and so forth. But these thoughts are energized to attract people, circumstances, and material items. When you use the law to call forth something, it will come to you provided the thoughts are not half-hearted wishes. With the law of attraction, anything is possible. This is the same idea that's true when working with the angels. Anything is possible. Use your mind. Focus it clearly on what you want. Have a feeling of worthiness to have what you want. Cultivate the intention to have it. Believe that the manifestation of what you desire is already possible and in the works to come to you. Know the law of attraction is continually responding. It responds to what you think, desire, and feel. In keeping with the law of attraction, try using an affirmation to call the angels to you.

Raising your vibration is empowering yourself by changing your thoughts from the negative to the positive. You can do this by writing or saying an affirmation. An affirmation is declaring the truth through a positive statement. For example, if you are continuously saying, "There must not be angels because I cannot see or feel them," change that statement and affirm, "I know there are plenty of angels here for me. I am willing to see and feel their loving presence." In essence you are raising your vibration to experience the possibilities of the angelic realm. If your thoughts are filled with fear and doubt, you will continue to experience the same. As you think so shall it be. In essence, you need to fake it until you make it through the use and power of affirmations. When you practice using affirmations, you shift your thoughts to experience what you want versus what you don't want. It creates a power that opens the gateways to experience miracles.

AFFIRMATION TO ATTRACT ANGELS

State your affirmation in the positive and in the present tense. For example, you do not say "I will see the angels someday." This statement keeps it in the future tense. Instead, speak the truth: "The angels are here and I am opening myself to perceiving them. I can ask of them anything for my highest good, so I request (state your request, such as, their visible presence or a sign), and I give thanks, knowing that my angels are already in the process of manifesting my request."

23: Send out Your Soul Call to the Angels

Your deep, abiding desire to meet the angels can magnetize your summoning them. You have heard the old phrase, "When the student is ready, the teacher appears." Just so, when you are ready—that is, when your heart is open and your mind is available to not only take in new information but to process what might come from the angels—that is when the angels are most likely to respond in a way that you can know they are definitely hearing you.

Have patience as you cultivate a relationship with the angels. You may desire specific results to occur in an instant, and because of factors that might be beyond your control, reaching your goal takes longer. Eschew the need for instant gratification. During restless moments, pray for patience, keep the faith, and believe the angels are working behind the scenes. Ask the angels to empower you with patience and perseverance, and trust that your desire is coming to fruition.

If you want to increase your intuitive abilities so you can communicate with the angelic realm, study and learn as much as you can. Your desire and motivation creates the energy of enthusiasm that is like a magnet, drawing to you everything that you need to develop your skills.

It's important to understand that the angels communicate with you through your database of information and knowledge. So as you expand your knowledge and you enhance your intuition, they have more ways to communicate with you. For example, if the angels see that you are paying attention to coincidences and synchronicities, then they will use this method of communication to get your attention.

When you ponder a focused desire (such as calling the angels in meditation or even writing them a letter), the angels will make things happen. Start by having a heart-to-heart dialog with your angels to open the lines of communication. Talk to the angels as if you were talking to your best friend and share with them your deepest desires and wishes. Remember, they already know who you are and everything there is to know about you. They are excited to make the connection with you and to help you in any way they can.

24: Surrender Your Prayer to the Angels

By now, you have learned that the number one priority in working with the angels is to ask for help. Once you do this and your request is made, you need to trust and surrender your prayer to God and the angels. This can be hard for some people who have a hard time letting go of control. If this applies to you, contemplate this thought: Do you trust that God and the angels have your best interest in mind? If so, it's time to surrender.

A wonderful way to surrender is to find or create a surrender box. Another name for it can be your "let go and let

God box." Place all your desires, wishes, and intentions into this box and then affirm, "I am letting go and letting God. I am open to my highest and best, better than I could ever imagine." By performing this ritual, you release your intentions from your control and you give them to God and the angels for miracles to occur. You break free from your human limited thinking, and you open up to the unlimited possibilities of divine resolution to occur. Once you surrender, it's your job to trust. Release your expectations and trust that everything is in divine order. God will take care of the all the details.

A final word about expectation is to expect the best outcome. Always. It is your natural birthright to connect with God and the angels. When the veil is lifted between heaven and earth, there is no separation between you, the angels, and God. You are a child of God, and because of your heritage you always have access to the divine. You can receive clear communication with God and the angels, and you can tap into the divine wisdom where all knowledge is found.

25: Fine-Tune Your Senses for Supernatural Receptivity

Your senses are extremely important in the development of your psychic or intuitive powers. They are also important to your ability to detect paranormal activity, and your ability to participate in spiritual practices that develop a greater receptiveness to supernatural phenomena. An archangel or enlightened master could appear at the foot of your bed in the middle of the night and exude an exotic incense aroma as he or she draws near. If you have been attentive to various scents in the months, weeks, or days preceding the nighttime visitation (and perhaps also burning incense, meditating, praying, walking in nature, or summoning angels or others from the higher celestial realms), you may in fact be getting what you asked for. If you awaken to the scent, you might move toward the spot where the scent seems to be emanating, and discover that shifting your head to the left or right a few degrees means you can no longer detect the scent; moving back, you rediscover it. This type of scenario of an angel visitation is not unusual when you have fine-tuned your sense of smell. But such a visitation could also manifest as a being of light, or soft and repeated brushes against your skin, or other unusual physical sensations.

There are numerous techniques to develop your receptivity to psychic phenomena. One way is to use breath and visualization techniques combined with meditation.

A MEDITATION ON LIGHT AND PEACE

When doing any of the meditations throughout this book, it's a good idea to record the session. Then you can easily let go to experience the meditation, versus opening and closing your eyes to read the next step. This will enhance your meditation and allow you to go deeper into the experience. Take your time recording, and remember to pause between each step.

Find a quiet place to sit where you will not be disturbed. You can do this meditation in silence, or play soft meditative music in the background.

- Get as comfortable as you can, and close your eyes.
- Inhale deeply, and with the exhalation, let go of every concern or negative thought.
- Take another deep breath, and release all the tension in your body.
- Now breathe into the present moment, and just let go.
- Form an intention in your thoughts to have the angels come and surround you in a circle of light and protection.
- Imagine the room filled with divine white light and energy.
- Breathe that divine light in and out.
- Affirm that your angels are present, encircling you.
- Remember you are never alone, and you are loved.
- Imagine the brilliance of the sun before you. This sun is the energy of the Divine and the Heavenly Host.
- Imagine that you have a plug in the region of your solar plexus (just like a lamp has a plug to connect to an electrical source), and you are plugged into that brilliant, spiritual sun.

- Inhale the energy and light from this sun into your body, and imagine every cell illuminated with the sun's light.
- Imagine that you can then breathe the divine wisdom and guidance that you are searching for into your mind. The light illuminates your interior and exterior worlds.
- Feel enlightened, as if it were possible to merge with the divine mind as you merge with light and peace.
- Remain in the light of God. Be still. Feel at peace. Experience the love. It is yours and it always has been. (Pause.)
- Think of a question you would like answered by divine guidance, and ask it.
- Wait expectantly and patiently for the answer from the angels.
- Say thank you. To return, just take some nice deep breaths and begin to feel your body; feel yourself back in the room.

Remember, you can plug into this holy place of divine light and guidance any time you choose. Each and every time you do, you reconnect with the divine wisdom and healing that's rightfully yours.

26: Hone Your Psychic Skills

For centuries, Indian yogis have concentrated on spiritual development, engaging in penances; doing charitable deeds; meditating often and deeply; performing *anusthans* (special spiritual practices to gain a boon or blessing); chanting (sacred chants, most often in Sanskrit while keeping track on a *japa mala*, or string of holy beads); and performing daily *pujas* or rituals of worship—all toward the goal of spiritually evolving. In the process, they have discovered that the time spent in such practices awakens the latent power inherit in a person's etheric or spiritual body. As the energy centers or chakras are awakened, meaning vibrating at a higher speed, these centers' powers are activated, opening the way for the expression of a heightened level of intuition. The development of intuition is desirable if instant access to such incredible powers keeps you anchored on the spiritual path to enlightenment. The yogis, however, know that the blessing can also be a curse if the powers are used for non-spiritual, purely selfish, and negative purposes (which bring bad karma).

It is important to always stay focused on the higher beings of light and love—the angels, archangels, and other beings whose affinity is for the divine and whose purpose is to do the will of the Divine.

27: Practice "Noticing"

Before addressing the ideas you might pick up as part of divine guidance, it might be helpful to think about the differences between spirituality and religion (as they relate to interpreting divine guidance). Religion offers a specific set of beliefs and rules for people to follow and be inspired by. Spirituality is more about your own personal relationship with the divine. Religious dogma might dictate an avoidance of all things psychic or paranormal. Certain spiritual practices will incorporate a suspension of disbelief about the celestial world and contact between beings of that world and the human species. Religion and spirituality can merge or diverge; neither is right or wrong, good, or bad. There are many pathways that will lead you back home to God, where you can feel a deeper connection with the divine.

Begin noticing the details of your environment, especially in your physical sacred space where you have invited angel contact, but also at work or when you are spending time in your home, in your yard or garden, at the homes of friends, at church, at school, or elsewhere. And just as you notice the minutiae of your outer world, increase your powers of observation of the inner world; notice such details as the subtle sounds you hear, hot and cold sensations or points of pressure along your spine where the energy vortexes are found in the ethereal body, any unusual tightness in your throat or heat at the throat chakra, colored or clear light before your inner vision, and so forth. Here are some other possible intuitive, or psychic, impressions or details you might receive as divine guidance:

- The angels might show you a past memory from childhood as an answer to a prayer.
- You might hear the angels giving you directions while you drive to avoid an accident ahead. For example, "slow down," or "move over to the right."
- You might get a sick feeling in your stomach when you meet a new business associate, a sign that aligning in some way with that person might not be healthy for you or the business.
- You might see your future home or future soul mate in detail during your meditation.
- You might have a dream about a past life that is giving you insight into a present situation.
- You might get a feeling that someone is going to pass into heaven very soon, or perhaps you will have a dream with many symbols such as a coffin, graveyard, headstone, and the like that suggest death (although such symbols might also mean death of an old way of seeing something).

If you begin to receive these intuitive or psychic impressions and you feel nervous about getting this information, ask your angels to comfort you. They will reassure you that everything is okay. You would not be receiving this information if it wasn't meant to be. If you are unsure about the information, ask the angels to give you confirmation that this information is coming from a divine source. They will do everything in their power to make you feel comfortable and safe.

28: Consider Angels' Influence on Synchronicity and Coincidence

Synchronicity is a term that means a coincidence of events that appear to be related but not obviously caused by either one. Another way to think of it is that the word coincidence is actually two words, *co* and *incidence,* which means when two things happen at the same time for no apparent reason. The meaning is very similar to that of synchronicity. When you experience a synchronicity, it is coincidence with meaning or significance. You can enter into a flow of life where coincidences and synchronicities become your clues, leading you to the answer to your prayers. The angels are always working behind the scenes in your favor. Sometimes it's through coincidences, synchronicity, or even gentle nudges. For example, you're stuck and you need a sitter for the kids. You pray to the angels for help, and minutes later your friend calls and offers to take your kids. Who knows what caused this intervention? Maybe the angels planted your name in her thoughts so she would call you. If you would like to notice angel nudges, try the following affirmation.

AFFIRMATION FOR AWARENESS OF ANGEL NUDGES

Dearest angels, Please engage and hold my attention to show me what I need to know. Help me to see, hear, and experience the miracles of your love and guidance throughout my day. Thank you.

The angels may try to reach you through both synchronicity and coincidence, or they may work simply through a sign or gentle nudge that can be of almost any nature. Some of the ways you might notice angels at work trying to get your attention are as follows.

- The angels are reassuring you that something you deeply desire is coming to you. Example: You finally notice the billboard on the way to work has changed and the new message aligns ironically with something you want in your life.
- The angels are trying to get your attention. Example: You keep finding dropped dimes all around the house in the most obscure places.
- The angels are reassuring you that you are not alone. Example: You have asked the angels to make their presence known to you, and you see angel pictures and statues wherever you go.
- The angels are trying to point you in the direction that will lead you to your highest and best life. Example: You have asked the angels if it's in your best interest to

go back to school and get your degree, and that same week you receive a brochure in the mail from the college you were considering.

- The angels are answering a prayer. Example: You ask the angels to send you the perfect lawyer to help you through your tax audit; you meet someone at an event and she shares that her husband is a tax attorney.

- The angels are encouraging you to move forward toward meeting your needs and achieving your dreams. Example: Your family has grown and you are looking for a bigger house, but you're nervous about making the changes. You have been looking in a particular neighborhood, a "For Sale" sign goes up, and the realtor's name on the sign is Maria Angell.

Such coincidences and signs are confirmations to you from the angels. In fact, you can ask the angels to provide a sign when you want to validate their presence in your life.

29: Find Optimum Times and Frequencies to Work Closely with Your Angels

To work more closely with your angels, notice what is ironic or synchronous about everyday events. Notice when synchronous events happen, and how often, because the more you notice, the more they multiply. If synchronous events or coincidences seem to occur at certain times of the day, ascertain what conditions prevail at that time. Are you alone when the events take place? Are they occurring right after your meditation or prayers? Are you more open, peaceful, or alert at those times? Is that period a peaceful one that possibly precedes work hours that are stressful and energy depleting? Do the events occur when you feel most trusting? The following helpful hints enable you to track synchronous events as they show up in your life.

TRACKING SYNCHRONOUS AND COINCIDENTAL EVENTS

- If your schedule is jam-packed, ask the angels to work with you, and establish a particular hour of the day for angel signs, coincidences, and synchronous events to occur. Let the angels know that a particular hour is optimal for you.
- Watch to see what occurs during that hour. Do remember, however, that everything happens according to divine timing when the elements are in place, and whatever happens is for the good of all. Ask for a specific sign, such as a feather, a rose, or something that happens in a series of three. Specificity helps to ensure the sign you receive is from your angels.
- Keep turning your problems over to the angels, asking for help and signs.

- Write the time and date of any angel signs, coincidences, and synchronous events on a calendar or in a journal.
- Do not be disheartened if you fail to notice signs, and remember that the angels' work goes on behind the scenes. The angels may want you to contemplate something a bit more, and there might be a better direction they want you to explore. Cultivate trust and patience.
- As you notice events that seem synchronous during that hour of the day, and also at other times, see them as validating your ever-stronger ties with the angels.
- Thank the angels for the communication.

Realize that such signs are gifts from God, and He is saying that you are not alone. You have God and an army of angels to help you. Just ask for what you want and need. Then open your awareness, and expect the miracle of receiving your sign.

30: Practice the Art of Communicating with Loved Ones Who Have Passed Away

Necromancy is an old word (it is found in the oldest texts of the Bible), and according to Merriam-Webster means, "the conjuration of the spirits of the dead, for purposes of magically revealing something about the future or influencing the course of events." Perhaps you long to discuss a burning question, or you seek to chat to gain insight into a problem with a beloved relative, a friend, or much-admired teacher, but that person has passed over. With the help of your angels, you can communicate with the spirits of those who have passed through the veil separating the world of matter and the world of spirit. These spirits may even be trying to contact you. Perhaps they want to talk with you as much as you desire to speak with them. And if you do want to talk with a deceased person, know that you are not alone. Dr. John Stanton, author of a book about talking with the dead, noted that studies suggest that roughly 720 million people around the world every day talk to the dead. He was interviewed by *Weekly World News,* and explained that anyone can master the technique if they give it about five minutes of practice each day. Here's how.

1. Rest in a quiet place. Close your eyes and release all fear and worry. Ask your angels to surround you in a protective white light and keep vigil over you through the process.

2. Focus with your mind's eye on the person so that you hold a clear mental image of him or her.

3. Ask a clear and concise question. Ask for the answer and wait for it. Do not force a response. Just wait until it comes.

Some people feel and experience their loved ones who have passed on as their guardian angels. Their presence and love never leaves you, and yes, it can feel as if they are still around you and acting as your guardian angel. As mentioned before, the angels have never been in a physical form. They are celestial beings of pure light, love, and energy.

People who have crossed over and who are now in the spirit world are better referred to as spirit guides. Some loved ones may choose, as part of their soul plan and evolution, to be a spirit guide for you during your life's journey. It is said that the relatives you were named after at the time of birth have a soul contract to watch over you as spirit guides after their transition to the other side.

Always show respect and gratitude, not only to the souls who have passed over who may communicate with you, but also to the angels for their loving, protective presence.

31: Consider a Consultation with a Psychic if You Need Help

If you are interested in communicating with your loved ones in spirit but would like to have someone more skilled in dealing with paranormal work than you are, go ahead and seek an experienced medium. They have natural abilities, or they have developed their skills to communicate with that world. Their job is to deliver evidential information and messages of love proving the continuity of life after death. This information can be very healing, and it can bring peace to those who are missing their loved ones.

Thoughts from the divine flow from the highest level of the One Consciousness through heavenly realms (virtual reality), through the quantum realm, and finally to the material world of vibration that you inhabit. Such things as stress, perpetual activity, lack of focus, emotional turmoil or shock—in short, anything that happens in the course of an ordinary day of your life—could conceivably block that flow. To restore peaceful thoughts and feelings of harmony that come from contact with the One Consciousness, you will need to move your thoughts away from stress, lack, worry, fear, and emotional turbulence. Follow any of these tips after first asking the angels to help you remove anything that might be hampering the divine guidance you seek or blocking peaceful or inspired thoughts.

- Listen to inspirational music.
- Lift your heart to God through inspirational reading.
- Reflect on spiritual concepts over a cup of herb tea.
- Let your mind drift in peace on birdsong.
- Dive more deeply into meditation.
- Sink into a gentle reverie preceding sleep but while you are still awake.

As your brain adapts to new ways of thinking, opens to new perceptions and receives new impressions, you may at times feel overwhelmed, and whether you do it consciously or not, you may obstruct or otherwise hamper the flow of incoming angel messages and information. If you feel that after trying to work with the angels you are not getting the results you had hoped for, then it might be the time to consult an angel intuitive that can help you find a way to break through any blockages. Since few people share the same skill levels, rely on recommendations to find someone you can trust. Local city park and recreation departments sometimes have psychic workshops, or you might find such classes through local New Age bookstores. Also consider praying to Archangel Michael. Use the following prayer or make up your own.

PRAYER TO RELEASE NEGATIVITY

Archangel Michael, please release me from all negativity and heal me right now. Release me from the negativity of others. Release my energy from anyone I fear. (Imagine that everyone is unplugging from you, and you are unplugging from others.) Archangel Raphael, God's healer, please restore my energy with green emerald healing light (imagine all your cells illuminating in green emerald healing light), and please send healing to all others involved. Thank you, Archangel Michael and Raphael, for your loving assistance.

32: Keep Your Angel Questions Simple, Initially

Imagine the excitement you will feel knowing that it is possible to receive guidance from the angels through life's thorniest issues, gain insights into how to have your best life right now, and manifest your heart's deepest desires. It is not only possible, it is reality that you can test and see for yourself. It would be easy to go a little crazy and start asking questions with multiple parts. Don't. Instead, keep your questions as simple and clear as possible. Feel surrounded in a bubble of angel light. Feel strong and centered, because that is what comes when you are in close contact with the angels. Transmute any negative energy into positive anticipation, and you will be empowering yourself and everyone around you. Transform your fears into faith. Pose your simple requests. Believe that your requests have been heard and are in the process of being answered. Jesus said, "And all things, whatsoever, ye shall ask in prayer, believing, ye shall receive" (Matthew 21:22). As you become more adept at clear communication with your angels (and also more convinced that your prayers are always heard and being answered), your questions can become more complicated. Simple and clear is the best strategy to follow in any communication, especially when talking with the angels or during your prayers.

Part 4

USE VARIOUS SPIRITUAL TOOLS TO CONTACT ANGELS

Legions of angels stand at the ready to serve you in countless ways, and you have spiritual tools through which to contact the angels. For example, a prayer is a request to God for help. As God's helpers, angels may be dispensed, either alone, in smaller numbers, or in an army. Sometimes they are dispensed to answer a soul call for comfort, a complicated question, a heartfelt request you make for another person, and so forth. A single angel may be sent to deal with the problem, or a legion may be sent. Numbers matter not, and it is not for you to know how the Divine goes about the work in order to help with physical and emotional problems, and even the healing of relationships and pets. If it's physical or emotional healing you need, the angels will surround you with loving, healing energy and empower you to connect with your own inner healer. If you need outside support from others, they will connect you with the right people or resources you need to help you achieve health and wholeness. If you are in pain, they will provide comfort and peace to help ease that pain.

For angel help in your relationships with others, the angels may ask you to practice forgiveness, they may encourage you to communicate and express your feelings, or they may even give you peace of mind and heart if you need to let go of a toxic relationship.

The angels are there in assistance for all of God's creations, including animals. You need only send your call for help to the angels, and they will come. Some of the tools you can use to call them include praying, dousing for answers, studying the symbols of certain types of cards, and engaging in rituals that you create.

33: Read Scripture and Prayers to Invoke Angel Response

There is no formal way to ask angels to make their presence known to you. You can simply call out to the angels by name, or you can say, "Angels, gather around me and surround me in your love." Then ask for whatever you need. No prayer is too small or too large. Surrender your prayer to divine resolution, and trust that your prayer has been heard and will be answered in divine timing. Try the following technique.

CALLING ALL ANGELS INVOCATION

Call an angel by name, or keep it more general. Close your eyes, hold out your arms and hands in an open embrace, and say, "Angels, gather around me and surround me in your love." Then ask for whatever you need. Fold your hands together as if in prayer and wait to see if there might be an immediate response. Remember that the magnitude or size of a prayer does not matter to God and the angels. No prayer is too small and insignificant or too large. Surrender your prayer to divine resolution, and trust that your prayer has been heard and will be answered in divine timing.

34: Douse for Angel Answers Using a Pendulum

Dousing, the ages-old technique of using a forked sapling or tree branch to find water, has also been used to answer yes and no questions (bouncing or moving in one direction for an affirmative answer and bouncing in the opposite direction for a no). Similarly, the same type of process works with a crystal suspended by cord or a fine-mesh chain from a bead. Dousing is easy and particularly helpful when your angels need a simple way to signal their yes/no responses to your questions.

Imagine a bead fastened to a four-inch chain from which dangles a multisided crystal in the shape of a triangle, its point aimed toward the ground. As you hold the pendulum still (after you have slid the bead between two fingers and allowed the pendulum on the chain to freely dangle), you will notice it beginning to move in a circular motion. Tell your angels which direction indicates a "yes" answer (for example, clockwise) and which direction means a "no" (counterclockwise). Tell your angels that any answer they cannot reveal or that is not yet known will stop the pendulum. That way, there will be no confusion about the answers the pendulum reveals to the questions you ask. The crystal, when magnetized by your energy and the blessing of angel energy seems to swing on its own. In fact, some dowsers claim the crystal moves entirely by itself, others assert that it rotates as a result of the energy flowing through the person holding the pendulum.

But for those who share a belief in angels, it seems plausible that the angels move the pendulum through influence over the holder's energy and thoughts.

Quantum physics studies indicate that the universe is energy, you are energy, your thoughts are energy, and everything else is energy. Everyone has the energy centers, or chakras (like wheels with spokes) and *nadis,* or nerves, running through the ethereal body like a nervous system. They work as transmitters of energy. When your chakras are balanced (not blocked or unbalanced) and your intuitive senses are heightened, you are in the best attunement to the energy of God and the angels. In this flow of consciousness, you can gain clarity and receive messages of divine guidance through the medium of spiritual tools such as a dousing crystal.

AN EASY DOUSING TECHNIQUE

1. Hold the crystal pendulum between your palms to charge it with your energy.
2. Invite the angels to bless the pendulum so that it will serve only your highest good as it provides the answers to your questions.
3. Stretch out your right hand so the palm is facing toward the floor, place the bead end of the chain through two fingers, and simply hold, allowing the chain and pendulum to drop.

4. Cup the other hand's open palm beneath the pendulum (as if to catch it). Hold the palm open and close to the crystal, but do not touch it.

5. Call your angels and demonstrate for them how you want the crystal pendulum to swing for a yes answer (clockwise) or a no answer (counterclockwise).

6. Focus on your question. Do not force the pendulum to move. It will move through the energy of the angels and your energy.

7. Ask the angels your question, and wait and watch for their answer through the swinging of the crystal.

35: Work with Angel Cards

Angel card decks, available in bookstores and on the Internet, serve as powerful spiritual tools for clarification of messages from the angels because each card in the deck contains images and words designed for that purpose. Such cards provide insight into the roles angels play and how they assist you. Most of the decks are packaged with a book that gives a description and detailed information about each card along with a message of divine guidance. A theme common of most angel cards, also known as "oracle cards," is the power of positive thought. Angel cards are similar to divinity tarot cards, however, they do not include any of the darker images that are found in the fortune-telling tarot decks. The following list suggests several ways to become familiar with angel cards.

TIPS FOR USING ANGEL CARDS

- Read the entire booklet that comes with your deck. It describes each card and its significant meaning.
- Pick one card at a time, and learn the meaning of that card.
- Pick a card. Before you read the booklet, write to the angels and ask them for the message and meaning of each card. (After you've finished writing, you can always go back and see what the book says.)
- Pick a card and place it by your bedside or under your pillow. Ask the angels to teach you the meaning of the card during your dream state.

Becoming familiar with individual cards, learning the card meanings, and being able to make relevant inferences or deductions for your questions, dreams, and meditations based on the cards enables you to interpret what you see more fully. Combined with thoughtful analysis of the communication you are receiving through other means from the angels, the cards become one more tool for clarity. Use angel cards to elucidate angel information from other sources about relationships, finances, health, emotions, life purpose, career, family and child issues, or legal issues. Working with the cards can yield insights. Whether or not card messages make immediate sense (as with dreams unfolding, it may even take a few days for the meaning to become clear), take the time to persevere when working with the cards. The following list suggests possible results of an angel card reading.

- The reading may reveal an immediate answer to a prayer.
- The reading may suggest that you need to make some changes in your life.
- The reading might initiate healing: physical, emotional, mental, or spiritual.
- The reading might open your awareness so you can pay attention to the angels.
- The reading might provide you with the help and guidance you are seeking.
- The reading may indicate the direction you need to go to achieve some goal, or it may reveal information that has remained obscure or unavailable to you.
- The reading may provide you with a feeling of peace: that you are right where you are meant to be, and all is well. After you have learned to decipher the meanings of the angel cards, why not try a past-present-future reading? Perhaps you desire to know what your future holds, but equally important is the understanding of how choices and situations in the past continue to influence and impact the present and future. The greatest gift you can give yourself from a past-present-future reading is to learn from the cards, and see new direction for living your best life now in the present moment.

Follow these steps to perform an angel-card reading, to receive insight about your past, present, and future:

PAST-PRESENT-FUTURE READING

1. Take the steps you've learned for preparing for an angel reading. Ask your angels to surround you in divine white light and energy before picking your cards.

2. Hold your deck of cards in your hands and say a prayer asking to receive insight and guidance about your past, present, and future in order to better open yourself to the working of the divine in your life and be guided to all opportunities, relationships, and situations for your highest good.

3. Spread your cards out on the table. Then breathe, and ask your angels to help you pick the perfect cards. The first card is about the past. Choose your card and place it face side up. The second card is about something significant or something you need to know about your present life. Choose your card and place it to the right (it will be your middle card). The last card is about your future and this card gets placed to the right of your present card. All cards can be faced right side up.

4. Take a few minutes to look at your spread of cards, and ask the angels for guidance. Listen, feel, and ask

for the clarity you need. Use the book enclosed with your deck of cards to discover even more detail and trigger more ideas.

5. Close the reading by thanking your angels, and ask them to continue to guide you so you may fully understand the significance of your reading.

6. Write or photograph the spread. If some of your cards don't make sense at the time of the reading, review them at a later time. Trust that you will receive exactly the spiritual insights you seek.

Each card shares a message or a story for your edification that illuminates various aspects of your life in some way. The "past" card reveals information from your past that could help you heal or better your life in the present and the future. Your "present" card asks you to pay attention to what's happening in your life right now. Your "future" card is sending you a message about a future opportunity or healing.

It is always important to use discernment when doing a card reading. If the cards you pick don't feel right or if you really don't understand the meaning of the cards, then reshuffle the cards again and pray with the angels and ask for help in picking new cards. Such a reading can be a blessing when you desire clarity or need help with a troubling situation or problem. Armed with a wider perspective, a reading can empower you to make better decisions, take appropriate action, or pay closer attention. Most often, you will finish your reading with a sense of peace and understanding.

36: Read Angel Messages in Tarot Cards

Just as picking an angel card for a single-card reading is a fun way to connect with your angels and an insightful way to receive a message of divine guidance, so you can also choose a single card from a tarot deck. Whether you have a specific question; seek options, solutions, and ideas; hope to validate yourself for a decision; or you desire swift insight into the forces that may be surrounding a problem or issue, pick a card to answer a specific question or ask for the knowledge you require in that moment.

Like the angel cards, tarot cards are usually packaged with a book that reveals the meaning of each card's symbols. Questions you pose can be simple open-ended questions or more specific. For example, "What do I need to know today?" or "What do I need to know about (something specific)?" Some specific tarot cards have imagery and symbolism that is darker than the cards of an angel deck, however, even the darkest cards of a tarot deck can be interpreted in positive ways. For example, the "Tower" card suggests not the literal falling of a tower but rather the breakdown of structures to make way for something new; the "Death" card seldom means literal death but rather symbolizes transformation; and the "Devil" card suggests deception of some kind surrounding the question—a good thing to know, depending on what the question is and the circumstances surrounding the asking of that question. It is a cautionary card advocating the use of discretion in business and personal matters. The popularity of tarot in modern culture has spawned many different types of tarot decks, and you might even try a free reading at *www.facade.com/tarot*.

Follow each step to do a one-card reading using a tarot deck:

1. Remember, always ask your angels to surround you in energy and the white light of the divine before you pick a card.

2. Hold your deck of cards in your hands, and say a prayer to receive a message that will guide you to your highest and best, better than you could ever imagine. (If you are asking a specific question, state the question and ask that you be guided to the best card that will answer your question.)

3. Spread your cards out on the table. Then breathe and ask your angels to help you pick the perfect card. You can always look at the cards and see which card jumps out at you, or you can pass your hand slowly across the cards. Feel through the energy in your hands, and notice where your hand is drawn to, then pick that card.

4. After you select your card you might have a clear meaning of what the card is telling you. If not, read the book that comes with the deck, or ask the angels to help you understand what it means.

5. Thank your angels, and ask that they continue to guide you.

Enjoy your journey while working with your angel deck. Witness your connections deepen between yourself, God, and the angels, and allow the cards to guide you to the answer to your prayers.

It may seem as if the card you selected doesn't have any significant meaning. If this happens, write down the card that you picked in your journal, and stay in tune with the angels. Pay attention during the upcoming week. Most likely, the card's meaning will be revealed in the next couple of days or by the end of the week.

37: Invite Angels to Communicate Through a Ouija Board

The Ouija board, once an innocent pre–World War I parlor game favorite, evolved into a popular divining tool, used by spiritualists, in the twentieth century. Although many people see it as a device for accessing information of a spiritual nature that remains hidden until exposed through use of the board, it is important to note that some Christian religions and others who believe in magic, witchcraft, and supernatural phenomena eschew its use because of associations of the Ouija with earthbound spirits, lost souls, and the like. However, if you have summoned your angels, surrounded yourself in the pure white light of the divine, and asked explicitly for the protection of the archangels and your guardian angels, and requested that only your angels communicate with you through the Ouija, using the board would be very much like writing numbers 1 through 9 along with the alphabet on a chalk board and asking your angels to spell out their messages to you (except you wouldn't be using a chalk board and chalk). The Ouija board contains the alphabet, the numbers, the words "yes" and "no" and "hello" and "goodbye." See it and use it as a tool that facilitates angel communication.

38: Welcome Angels Into Sacred Space Refined Through Feng Shui Principles

Create sacred space in which to regularly welcome the angels into your life, and further enhance the beauty and spiritual energy vibration of that space by utilizing some of the principles of feng shui, the ancient Chinese art of placement. Feng shui emphasizes the placement of shapes, colors, and symbols in ways to achieve balance, harmony, and pleasing aesthetics. For an indoor space, organize, clean, and clear the space of clutter. Removed items can be stored in boxes or baskets with lids but out of sight. The space should be clean with a few pieces of furniture to fit the scale of the room, soft textiles, furnishings (pillows, window dressings, oriental carpets, and cushions, for example), and a well-placed plant such as an orchid or a lush *dieffenbachia* (never plants with spiky, sword-like leaves because they symbolize strife and aggression). Hang a clear crystal by a red string in a window to catch the light, and add angel artwork such as a painting or statue. Let in the light—through the windows or better illumination of lamps, overhead lights, pendulum lights, or sconces. Use flower essences or oils to scent the space. A beautiful piece of stained glass positioned at a window could add interest, but must work with the rest of the objects in the room to increase the energy vibration.

Outside the front door, a melodious wind chime welcomes the angels, and according to feng shui principles, also brings prosperity into your home. Let the room be one in which you feel peaceful upon entering. The vibration in the room must necessarily be high to help you tune into angel energy. Think of this space as holy and blessed. It should make you feel special when you enter it as if you are there to welcome your unseen friends—the angels—who, with you, support your soul's purpose, reinforce your spiritual intentions, continue helping you to work on self-examination and knowledge, and maintain balance in all you do.

39: Decipher Signs, Symbols, and Significance

Perhaps you have had one of those days that leave you so tired, it is all you can do make it home and crawl into bed, even though you know there was something else you were supposed to remember to do today, but you didn't do it. You think you said some prayers, but you can't be sure because you were so tired. Then sometime in the middle of the night, you awaken from a dream and you smell the perfume of your deceased mother. It seems to be emanating from the foot of the bed. The scent has brought you out of sleep into wakefulness, and now you crawl to the foot of the bed. You see nothing, feel nothing, and yet there is that scent. Turning your head so your nose is to the left or the right, the scent is not there. It remains for a few moments and then dissipates. You crawl back to your pillow and lie in the dark, wondering what just happened. Then you remember that it is the anniversary of your mother's death, and you wanted to mark her passing by lighting a candle before bed. Too fatigued, you forgot.

When communicating with the angels, you soon learn to decipher such signs or symbols and their significance. During your dream state your ego gets out of the way, and it is easier for the angels to deliver messages of divine guidance. Knowing this, you can make a point of writing a specific question on a piece of paper and tucking it under your pillow before going to sleep. Ask your angels to give you guidance through the dream symbolism, and also ask that you are able to remember the dream upon awakening. Dreaming the dream and remembering are important if you are to unlock the message by deciphering the symbolism. Take heart in the knowledge that your angels can help with that too.

40: Align Your Desire with Divine Will to Attract Angels

God gave you the power to create. That is an amazing gift, especially when aligned with divine will. When you set an intention, pray over it, affirm it, and take action to manifest it, the angels know and are ready to help when you call upon them. Think of a legion of angels with pursed lips blowing wind into your sails to set your ship on a course to create a magical life, and helping you to achieve everything you want when you align your will with that of the Divine. If your life isn't working and you do nothing, what is going to change? Perhaps it is time to start shifting to a new direction, and to set a new course. You can do it with the invisible force of the angels. Imagine how powerful you truly are, even during those times when you feel beaten down and impotent. You aren't really powerless and never were. You have God's power and his angels to help you create the life you want. And you can shift the energy at any moment, call out to the angels at any time, and start the process of change in a heartbeat. Things can happen very quickly when you yoke your will to that of the Spirit, of the Creator. Give it a try and see for yourself. Start by answering these questions.

- What would you change about your life, if you could?
- Where do you want to be by this time next year in your most important relationships? In your job or career? In your spiritual life?

- Where do you want to be living?
- Who is going to be living there with you?
- How much money do you desire to manifest by the end of the year?
- When do you want to retire? What kind of life will you have during retirement?
- What kind of physical and emotional health would you claim for yourself if anything were possible?

After you answer these questions, ask yourself, "What's holding me back from having what I want?" The bottom-line answer for that question is you—your thoughts, your worries, your fears—give those things up, and instead embrace the possibility of having what you want. Call on the angels for your wants and needs, and work with divine guidance to create a new life filled with what you desire, not what you lack or worry about.

41: Feel Deserving and Worthy of Interacting with Angels

You are a child of God and your natural birthright is to receive from the divine. Learn the difference between the thoughts and feelings coming from your ego and divine guidance in order to interact with the angels. You might find it helpful to read the following list of basic characteristics of the ego.

- The ego is judgmental.
- The ego is critical.
- The ego is indecisive.
- The ego procrastinates.
- The ego is impatient.
- The ego likes to control.
- The ego is fearful.
- The ego says you're unworthy and undeserving.
- The ego is competitive.

Notice your thoughts, and see if you can detect any of those characteristics as they pop into your mind. When you know that such thoughts come from the ego, you can choose to focus instead on the positive, uplifting, loving thoughts of the angels. Don't beat yourself up for having these thoughts. Simply say, "Here my ego goes again," and choose to take back your power.

42: Ask, Believing That the Answer You Seek Will Come

Because the voice of divine guidance always comes from a place of love, it will never lead you down a path of pain or chaos. Divine guidance asks you to follow your heart and to believe in your dreams and aspirations. Positive, helpful, healing, and supportive, the angels' messages will encourage you and provide you with the trust and confidence you need to

follow your heart. In simple terms, the voice of divine guidance is always the voice of love. Your job is to ask for help and
then to believe that not only has your request made its way
to heaven and the angels, but that it has been heard and that
the answer to your request is on its way to you. Believing the
answer you seek will come is an important part of the process.

When you hear the voice of your angels, it sounds like
this.

- "You are good enough right now."
- "Follow your heart."
- "Believe in yourself."
- "You can do anything if you believe."
- "You are never alone and you are so loved."
- "You are right where you are meant to be."
- "You deserve the best."
- "Be patient. All is well."
- "There is more than enough to go around."

43: Demonstrate Respect for All Things Divine

When you set out a crystal bowl, and place a fresh gardenia
bloom in it with a silent thank you to the angels, they know
you are showing respect. Or, when you light candles and
incense before beginning your meditation, and you offer a
welcome prayer to the angels, that too is a sign of respect. But

when a fly or moth flits around your altar table and you grab a swatter to put an end to it because it annoys you, it shows a wanton disregard for the life of those creatures. Think of the world and everything in it as made by the Creator; each thing has its own holiness. Flies and moths are not sentient beings aware of their own consciousnesses like humans are. In other cultures, the reverence for life is so great that people strive to avoid hurting other living creatures. In India for example, Jain priests (Jain being an Indian religious sect) wear masks in case they might inadvertently inhale a gnat or other insect, thus ending its life. Attuning your energy to the life force of other creatures fosters an understanding of the spark of divinity in all. Small, albeit sometimes annoying, creatures like flies and moths may seem useless, but in fact they have their place in the grand scheme of the divine. When you feel and demonstrate a loving respect for other life forms, your energy vibration becomes more attuned to the angels.

44: Express Gratitude to the Angels

Expressing gratitude to the angels can take many forms—a straightforward thank you will do, but also consider demonstrating your appreciation through your actions and good works. As you already have learned, the angel energy is energy of light, love, and respect. When you understand the inner connectedness of all things in the universe, you grasp the idea that a change in one thing affects change elsewhere. When

you are on your path, and working toward spiritual enlightenment, that can lift others. When you live in the spirit of
love and honor and respect for even the smallest, seemingly
insignificant beings, you are showing gratitude to God and
the Angelic Host for the blessing of life. As you live in closer
alignment with the heavenly beings, you cultivate positive
attitudes of joyfulness, loving kindness, serenity and peace.
That too is a way of expressing appreciation and gratitude.

Think about it for a moment—when you shun strife and
struggle (by calling on your angels for help)—and instead find
the harmony in your own life, that colors all your relationships. The subtle ripple effect, though intangible and unseen,
can actually lift the collective consciousness of those involved
with you. In ancient times, people offered sacrifices to show
their gratitude to the divine. In the New Testament, Jesus
demonstrated loving kindness through his acts and taught his
followers to live with an appreciation for what they already
had; He also taught them to trust that their father God knew
their needs. A life of loving service is one of the best ways to
thank God and the angels for the blessings you receive every
day.

Part 5

FIND THE BEST PLACES TO MEET YOUR ANGELS

Your angels don't really need a special place to meet. They are around you all the time, but having a special place where you can sit, pray, meditate, talk, chant, sing, or write without interruption can aid in quicker attunement with angel energy. When the dog is barking, the baby is crying, and your spouse is frantically searching for that misplaced item, you are not in the right frame of mind for angel visitation (although you can call upon them to quiet the dog and baby and show you where the misplaced item is hiding). It might take some exploring to find the best place to meet your angels—that place where you feel peaceful, gather your thoughts, and sink into deep reflection, meditation, and contemplation.

45: Invite the Angels Into Sacred Space

In truth, even when sitting at your computer, turning your attention to prayer for a short daily period can energize the surrounding area into a sacred space through the energy vibration of your intention and thought. Any place where worship or religious ritual is conducted spiritualizes that place. Sacred places are also sites of creativity and spiritual renewal. Religious anthropologist Mircea Eliade suggests that sacred spaces are places where spiritually transformative experiences that have particular meaning for humans take place. A safe place, away from the chaos, for God's peace and serenity to enter your life can be your desk in the home office or elsewhere. But when you have had an experience with the angels or with divine guidance, regardless of where it happened, that space most likely will be deemed sacred space. Your sacred space will most likely already be in your environment; this means you don't have to find a cave in the Himalayan mountains or a spot in an isolated village along the fringes of the Sahara Desert. Moses dropped to his knees on Mount Horeb. The Buddha sat under the Bodhi tree. Jesus often prayed in the Garden of Gethsemane. These places became sacred because of the transformations of those praying there. Your sacred space where you choose to invite your angels might even be at your computer. The point is to find a place, and extend the invitation to your unseen allies.

46: Visit Houses of Worship

Perhaps you are attracted to the great cathedrals in Europe, the hillside grottos of France and Italy, the miniature churches dotting the Greek islands, or the villages of Central America. Or you appreciate the quiet, spiritual sanctuary of your local Jewish temple, mosque, or church down the street. Houses of worship are great places to meet angels, especially if you often spend quiet time there. These places are always charged with the palpable energy of the devout who have been gathering there for years, sometimes centuries, to show devotion and engage in prayer and ritual.

After you choose your special place, possibly in some corner of a house of worship, set your intention that this is your special place to come where you can let go, pray, and be open to the gifts and miracles of the angels. Each and every time you enter your space, invite the angels to gather, and ask them to surround you in their loving light and protection. Ask them to fill your space with the highest vibration of divine white light and energy, and know that with every breath that you take, you will become one with this sacred healing light.

After you meditate, engage in intuitive exercises, or spend time in prayer anywhere, (but especially in houses of worship that others are using), remember to ask the angels to "zip up" your energy field. You don't want to walk around taking on (receiving) everyone's psychic information. You want to allow only the divine guidance meant for you and your highest good.

47: Pray in a Cemetery

Cemeteries are final resting places for souls who have completed their journey from life in a human body. Some people believe in a continuity of the human spirit and that when people pass away, they exist as spirits. Cemeteries, often adorned with angel statuary or angel images on headstones and benches, are places of serenity and solitude. Manicured lawns, graceful trees, and pretty shrubs and flowers such as roses and lilies can be seen in many such necropolises, or cities of the dead, as large cemeteries are known. Also, many cemeteries contain some of the most beautiful sculptures of angels, archangels, and spiritual symbolism in the world.

Angels gather in such places (and not only as stone and granite sculptures). In fact, there have been apparitions of angels and of the Blessed Virgin Mary in cemeteries such as the Queen of Heaven Catholic Cemetery in Hillside, Illinois (on August 15, 1990). The angel art in cemeteries is also inspiring. In Paris' famous Pere Lachaise Cemetery, some of the world's most beautiful and oldest angels have been photographed. Images from there are available in poster stores all over the world as well as through Internet sites. Just viewing some of the angels (using the *images* tag on Google) will undoubtedly lighten your heart and lift your spirits.

Many cemeteries bear the name of Mary, Mother of Christ or one of her many monikers. You may associate a cemetery visit with grief and sadness or disembodied spirits, but they are also places of light. You already know how to ask for angel protection and the light of the divine. Perhaps you know of a cemetery in your area where you could visit, and sit for a spell to invite the winged ethereal messengers—your angels—to join you.

48: Retreat to a Peaceful Garden

Gardens, havens of creative energy and new life, provide especially tranquil areas for meeting the angels. If you have access to such a place, go there often and invite the angels to join you. In San Jose, California, and other cities across the United States, the local municipality has established gardens for the community. San Jose maintains a spectacular rose garden and cultivates different varieties of roses, from hybrid teas to tree roses. Such lush and lovely gardens serve to "green up" urban America, and they have become an important part of city planning and urban renewal.

If you don't have access to such a garden or your community hasn't started a garden, why not create one in your yard where you and your angels can spend time in communion together? Your garden can be formal or informal; it is your choice. You can plant herbs, vegetables, flowers, berries, fruit trees, roses, and climbing vines, or include all of them in a French-style potager (kitchen) garden. You can plant in a way that creates a labyrinth (around which to do meditative walks), or cast the seed wherever and let it be a wild place. Hang wind chimes, place bird feeders around, and plant giant sunflowers to feed a variety of wild critters in the garden. Add a bench, a large stone, or a stump to sit on when you are not gardening and can talk with your angels.

49: Spend Time in a Monastery or near an Ancient Shrine

If you live near a monastery or facility that watches over an ancient shrine, take time to visit, and invite your angels to join you where you can convey thanks or ask for guidance or blessings. Some monasteries and convents welcome people to spiritually recharge on their grounds, but you do have to follow some rules. In some places, for example, silence must be observed during meals, and lights have to be out by a specific hour. Shrines the world over have been established because a holy and transformative event took place at the site, and shrines exist because of the spiritual love of the devout and the devotion of pilgrims intent on paying homage. Find ancient shrines, monasteries, convent grounds, and other such holy places where the devout worship, and there too will be angels.

When you believe you might need a spiritual retreat to quench the thirst of an arid heart, or to rejuvenate spiritual desire and longing for the divine and you feel that invisible pull on your heart, check in with your angels. If the guidance (or the vibration pull or attraction) isn't coming from your angels, it might be coming from spirit beings in even higher realms. Regardless of who is "calling" you to action, invite them along. Your angels will no doubt enjoy the vibration of the holy place you decide to visit. You too will enjoy the ambience and sacred hospitality you will likely find there. Just remember to focus on transcendence. Let the surroundings lift your spirit, but use the time you have during the retreat to nourish your inner world in order to deepen your faith and intensify your desire to live a richer life in spirit.

50: Hike to a Rock or Mountain Peak

Some people enjoy climbing rocks and scaling mountain peaks—the high they get is every bit as spiritual as diving deeply inward into blissful meditation. If you enjoy the outdoors and like scampering up cliffs, rocky crevices, or the sides of mountains, by all means go and do it. There is something sacred about standing atop a lofty peak and looking out to survey the world. There too you will find your angels. In fact, you can invite them to join you in every step of the process and ask them to be your guide, your sherpa, your protector, and navigator.

Combine your climb to a mountain peak with a period of devotion in a monastery, temple, or small church. It may come as no surprise that there are many sacred sites in the world where people have been worshipping for centuries in high places or along rocky promontories. For example, Orta San Giulio, Italy (site of the Santa Maria Assunta Church); the Yamunotri Temple in the lower Himalayan mountains of India; Mount Croagh Patrick, in County Mayo, Ireland; or the Temple of Poseidon, in Cape Sounion, Greece.

Jesus delivered one of his greatest moral teachings, the Sermon on the Mount, on a hilltop near Capernaum (*Nachum* in Hebrew) or possibly Mount Eremos (as it was known during biblical times). Moses talked with God on Mount Sinai; the great prophet of Islam (Muhammad) was visited by the angel Gabriel as the former meditated in a cave on Mount Hira, located near Mecca. Not only were these high places, they were also holy places—places where God spoke and the angels visited. Such places are often isolated and peaceful, and those are two excellent criteria to keep in mind when choosing suitable places for you to meet your angels.

51: Walk Into the Desert

If you live in America's arid west or southwest, you likely already appreciate the beauty and solitude the desert offers. There is something about the intensity of the desert landscape and the peace and quiet that draws you inward to align more closely with God and the angels. Jesus, according to the Gospel of Matthew, spent forty days and nights in the ancient Judean desert while the Devil tempted him, and at the end of that period was visited by angels: ". . . behold, angels came and ministered unto him" (Matthew 4:11). It is not surprising in that bleak environment that he found comfort in communion with the divine, in the company of angels. Unlike the heavenly choir that filled the heavens with their chorus to herald his birth, or the two who would sit at his tomb to announce that he had risen from death, these angels simply cared for him.

If you need the comfort of angels, walk into the desert and invite them to keep company with you. Ask them to assuage your fears, heal your heart, help you understand how to fix what isn't working in your life, protect you and your loved ones, and shelter you from the temptations that pull you in directions that are detrimental to your wellbeing and highest good.

52: Retreat Into the Temple of Your Heart

The most beautiful place to meet your angels is in the temple of your heart. By using your imagination and seeing with your mind's eye, this temple can appear in the style of ecclesiastical or other types of architecture that you most love, or it can appear simply as a natural setting with flowing water, blooming scented flowers, sheltering trees, verdant meadows, and a quiet cave or sheltered area. Imagine it any way you want that will draw you inward again and again. This imaginary place in your heart is hallowed space, made so because it is where you retreat from the cares of the world to commune with God and your angels.

If you like the idea of using a ritual to start the process of raising your vibration and preparing to meet your angels, conceive of a ritual that you will use each time you go into that temple. Your ritual might involve lighting a stick of incense before sitting or lying down, closing your eyes, and turning inward. Or it might involve sipping an herb tea from a special cup or placing a glass of water before you to be energized by the presence of angels (drink it afterwards). You could drink a little of the water before meditating to symbolize your consciousness sliding down into the inner recesses of your heart, symbolically opening the door of your temple. Or perhaps you close your eyes and visualize energy in a column rising through your chakra centers, along a channel extending from the base of your tailbone upward through the solar plexus (area of your kidneys) and navel to the heart chakra. As you see the energy column rise, imagine it passing through each chakra vibrating or whirling in the colors of red (at the tailbone), orange (at the solar plexus), yellow (at the navel), and green (in the heart). Rest in awareness there, or move your energy higher where you will see blue at the throat chakra, deep purple at the third eye, and violet at the crown. Whatever ritual you devise, use it whenever you are ready to spend time in your heart temple. You and your angels both understand that when the ritual begins, it is time to join together.

Part 6

EXPLORE WAYS TO COMMUNICATE WITH YOUR ANGELS

Some people give little thought to angels and divine assistance in their lives until facing a devastating crisis that compels them to initiate communication. Others, conversely, have cultivated such a personal ongoing relationship with angels that daily communication takes the form of chatting or mental conversation during mundane activities such as doing the dishes, feeding the dog, transporting the kids to soccer practice, or driving to work. How you communicate with your angels is your choice. Although most people associate any type of communication as either verbal, nonverbal, or written, you may prefer to have your contact be through mental prayer (interior prayer or contemplation, called by Saint Teresa of Avila a "close sharing between friends." Consider the value of each type of communication.

- Verbal—involves simply communicating your thoughts through speaking, whether in a whisper, chant, song, conversation, or joyful exclamation or shout.
- Nonverbal—adds richness to your communication through your "drawing near" in posture, forming and holding a meditative pose, leaning into a scent or energy field you believe emanates from the angels, folding your hands in prayer and bowing your head, or using your hands to offer something such as a flower or glass of water for the angels to charge with their energy. The latter might be an effective way to demonstrate respect and appreciation and to initiate or end communication with the angels.
- Written—possible to do anywhere using a variety of tools such as a pen, pencil, or paintbrush with paper, canvas, fabric, or glass; sticks for writing in sand; icing tubes for cake painting; a computer for making notes in an angel file; and chalk on a chalkboard, sidewalk, or masonry wall.
- Interior/Mental Prayer and Contemplation—does not require vocalization but best offered through focused and attentive awareness. The emphasis is not on thought so much as feeling love.

Your communication does not have to be overtly religious in tone, although many people find that feels most right for them. Saint Teresa of Avila, deemed a Doctor of the Church, believed that a simple prayer was best but contemplation was the highest form of prayer.

Always remember to say thanks for the love of the angels and the gifts and peace of mind they bring.

53: Have a Conversation with the Angels

Talking with your angels, as you have already learned, doesn't involve anything different than talking with your best friend, spouse, or confidant. When you reach out, your effort to open the channel of communication does not go unnoticed by the angels. They will respond to your open invitation by sending love, joy, and peace. If you are concerned about any area of your life, talk with them. If it helps to imagine your guardian angels seated at the table with you while you have your cup of morning coffee, start your conversation that way. Ask them to reveal to you their names. You can wait for inspiration, a name to pop into your mind, or an unusual occurrence that might reveal a name (such as a song on the radio that repeatedly evokes the name). You can talk about anything: finances, relationships, self-esteem, fears, motivation, depression, and virtually anything else. Once you have invited their presence and requested their help, you have to do three more things: surrender the problem to them (do not obsess about it, but instead release worry associated with it), trust that the angels are going to help you handle it perfectly and in the right time, and follow the direction that the angels give you. Their divine guidance can be revealed through your intuition or through coincidence such as a "chance" meeting or occurrence or in some other way.

54: Write to the Angels—in a Variety of Ways

If you love spending time on a beach, contact your angels there. Write an invitation in the beach sand, such as: "Welcome angels. Join me in this paradise." With a beach towel over your eyes and warm sand beneath you, you can sink into the right frame of mind to send out a mental telegraph to the angels, that you desire their presence. Lie still, meditate, pray, or just send out mental messages and wait for a response. Think of the angels as having the ability to imprint onto your mind the answers you seek. If you love baking for your family, bake an angel cake and use icing piping to write a message for the angels in the frosting. Also consider writing notes to your angels that you keep in a cookie jar or pretty vase. As the notes with your requests are answered through the work of your angels, jot down onto your written petition how the answer came, and then write a thank-you note to your angels. Write about your angels in a blog (making sure that you have asked them to connect with you through that blog). Or consider keeping an angel journal on the desktop of your computer, and log on each day to write down daily thoughts to share with them, problems that you face and would like their help solving, or the solutions that have taken place for issues for which you requested angel assistance. If you enjoy writing and needlepoint, why not use the time when you sit and work on a piece of embroidery (a work of angel art, perhaps) to knit a message of love to the angels?

55: Talk with Your Angels While Driving

Whether you drive or take public transportation to get from a departure point to your final destination, why not use that time to communicate with the angels? When driving, be careful not to get distracted by using a cell phone or texting; rather, focus on driving. Notice the roadway more, and everything associated with it, including the signs along that road. There may be divine guidance coming to you through billboard messages, license plates, detours, and street names, for example; the most important sense for driving and texting is sight. Texting or talking on a cell phone is considered a dangerous activity to do while driving. According to the National Safety Council that has completed more than 30 research studies on the subject, both tasks demand attention and cannot be performed together with optimum focus and effectiveness. However, chatting with a passenger such as your spouse, who is sitting with you in the car on the way to your relative's house, does not pose the same hazards. Likewise, communicating with your angels about your day is even less taxing on your brain; you can ask them to give you their responses at a later time. If you have a long commute and ordinarily think about your goals, hopes, dreams, and concerns, consider sharing those with your angels too. Also, ask them to protect you and everyone else on the road.

56: Make a Daily Appointment for Angel Communication

Why not make communication with your angels a daily commitment? In fact, if your life is tightly scheduled, pencil or type into your Blackberry or smartphone a daily time slot just as you would any other important appointment. It takes roughly twenty-one days to form a new habit, so keep that appointment without fail for three weeks. Watch as your life begins to change for the better.

Angel communication serves not only as a means for you to share the burdens of juggling career and family (or other obligations that weigh upon you), but also as a sounding board for creative ideas. How would you envision changing your life if you knew you had an invisible force of unseen assistants on whom you could call to create a new life or just change certain aspects of the one you already are living? If you knew you couldn't fail, would you strike out on your own, launch your own company, join the Peace Corps, or take a sabbatical from your career or studies?

In order to experience the presence of angels, turn off the electronic sounds around you. Instead, go to your spiritual center and listen to the beautiful natural sounds—a bird chirping, rain dripping, your own breath, or perhaps the flutter of an angel's wings or angel humming. Fortunately, it is not necessary to take up a hermit's life to experience the contemplative silence that is at the heart of experiencing the angelic world. You can achieve your own silence, and recognize the presence of angels by practicing silence on a daily basis.

57: Meet Your Angels in the Dreamtime

When you receive a vision or information about a future event, whether in a moment of sudden and profound lucidity, in deep meditation or in a dream, it's known as precognition. Many people have precognitive visions and dreams. You don't control the process. You simply become aware of that event, perhaps seeing it unfold or perceiving fragmentary information. Generally, you will perceive such a vision as being either positive or negative. If the vision pertains to death or disaster, such a vision can be quite upsetting. If you have a negative precognitive experience, ask the angels to help you feel comfortable with your ability so that precognition becomes a gift rather than a burden.

During your dream state your ego gets out of the way and therefore it's easier for the angels to deliver messages of divine guidance. Before you go to sleep, ask them to reveal the truth of what you believe you saw in the vision. Write a specific question on a piece of paper and put it under your pillow. Then ask the angels to communicate the answer to you through a dream and to help you remember the dream when you awaken. You can also ask your angels to help you dream again about the event if it is troubling or you seek greater insight. Sometimes, dream meaning isn't clear or easily deciphered from a jumble of seemingly unrelated symbols. You might want to experience the dream over a period of several nights.

58: Try Lucid Dreaming

Have you ever experienced a sudden awareness that you have "awakened" within your dream? Most likely, you were engaged in lucid dreaming. Images during lucid dreaming can be more vivid and clear than ordinary dreams. The lucid dream quality varies—you may experience a high level of lucidity (where you are not only aware that you are awake in the dream and can influence the direction of the dreaming but also you understand that the people in the dream are dream representations) or lower levels in which you know you have awakened in the dream and you can exert a little control over your dream course, defying the laws of physics, for example, to fly like your angels do.

Lucid dreaming offers an opportunity to discover the wonders of the world without physical limitations. You can enter a blissful state through thought and your thought forms also can manifest anything your mind can conceive. To learn more about lucid dreaming, read the works of Stephen LaBerge, PhD, psychophysiologist and an expert in the subject of lucid dreaming. The point of trying lucid dreaming is to provide yet another connection to your angels.

USING A TRIGGER TO INITIATE LUCID DREAMING

You can use the powerful experience of dream lucidity to communicate with your angels about specific areas of your life such as your relationships, health, finances, family matters, or spiritual and religious issues. Before sleep, ask your angels to help you to awaken while you are in a dream. Choose a trigger to become lucid—a clue that will remind you in the dream state that the angels are near and you are awakening while still dreaming. Examples of clues might include a key, harp, bird, airplane, or angel. Remind yourself throughout the day of this clue as your trigger to awaken. Call upon the angels and then sleep. Your dreaming mind and the angels will do the rest. Another simple technique is to awaken from sleep before you normally would, remain awake for a half an hour, and then return to sleep; these three steps together often trigger lucid dreaming. If you are like other people who have engaged in lucid dreaming, you will achieve more artistic inspiration, experience a greater sense of freedom, and do creative problem solving within your lucid dreams.

BENEFITS OF LUCID DREAMING

Have ever questioned the nature of reality? Ever wonder whether or not the world is a mental construct, not the "reality" of tangible things, but the reality of consciousness—only real because the mind perceives it so? Perhaps you desire to connect at the highest levels with the divine.

With the guidance of your angels, the opportunity to experience spiritual awakening and transcendence exists through lucid dreaming. Physical, mental and emotional healing can be achieved in lucid dreaming as well as the ability to interpret your dream even as it is happening, due to the conscious awareness and critical thinking ability of the brain that are engaged during a lucid dream.

59: Whisper to the Angels During Nature Walks

There's something magical walking in the dappled sunlight created by a leafy canopy of gnarled oaks and colorful maples, hiking along rows of lush vines and roses in a wine country vineyard, or strolling under a full moon with the heat of the day gone and the scent of wild thyme and scrub brush filling the air. Step into nature, and you enter the habitat of angels and fairies. In such natural settings, you may not desire to disturb the peace with normal vocalization, when a soft whisper will do. You may not see them, as according to many sources, angels and fairies can only be seen by humans if so deemed by the will of God. However, some people have the ability to see into the unseen realms and can discern spirits as the apostle Paul explained in his letter to the Corinthians about the many types of spiritual gifts: "Now concerning spiritual gifts, brethren, I would not have you ignorant . . . For to one is given by the Spirit the word of wisdom . . . To another the working of miracles;

to another prophecy; to another discerning of spirits . . ."
(1 Corinthians 12:10). Whether or not you have the gift of
"discerning spirits," if you would like to call forth the invisible
angels and fairies to accompany you in the enjoyment of nature,
make it part of your lifestyle to spend plenty of time outside
walking or just sitting, tuning into the company of angels. It is
the same glorious Power working through all spiritual gifts as
the apostle further observed, "But all these worketh that one and
the selfsame Spirit, dividing to every man severally as he will"
(1 Corinthians 12:11).

60: Send and Receive Messages in Meditation

You can utilize exercise (*hatha* yoga), concentration (*dharana
yoga*), and meditation (*dhyana* yoga) to refine the process of
getting into a quiet mental state. Meditation here is meant
as a state of being during which you can communicate with
the angels, not the techniques of yoga that you perfect to
get into that meditative state. Yoga is an ancient method
of linking your individual consciousness to that of the one
divine mind, and meditation is the seventh or penultimate
step in the eight steps of yoga outlined by the ancient Indian
sage Patanjali. After you have applied techniques to disconnect from the senses and turn inward, moving away from
ideas of mortal consciousness and all thoughts associated
with them, you rest in a state of peace and alert awareness in

the realm of spirit. That meditative state, in which you can dive ever more deeply into increasingly subtle realms, is the place to communicate to your angels. Initially you might use techniques of yoga to overcome mental restlessness, but eventually you will automatically sink into that meditative calm. Broadcast messages to the angels from your third eye center at the point between your eyebrows (*ajna* chakra) and receive their incoming messages in your heart chakra (*anahata* chakra).

61: Sing to the Angels

If you have ever felt your spirit grow lighter, your heart grow more joyful, and your worldly burdens disappear for a while as you listen to ecclesiastical or other beautiful music, you know its power. Some say the human voice is the most perfect instrument for music when chanting, humming, or singing sacred lyrics, especially when used with spiritually evocative words. Many churches, in fact, consider sacred song as a form of prayer.

Music as communal expression is probably one of the most effective means of using it. In the time of Jesus, Jews and the earliest Christians would have normally sung in the synagogues of that era. Only much later were prayers such as "Our Father" sung during church services. One of the earliest hymns that survives today is "O Gladsome Light" from the fourth century when it was mentioned by Basil the Great, an early Christian church father. If you desire contact with the angels, why not sing a hymn or prayer that you love as the means of watering an arid heart in preparation for sending out your soul call? Keep in mind, however, that singing can shorten your breath and excite your emotions. You want to calm the breath and subdue the emotions to reach the higher state of vibration to reach your angels. So sing, but remember to use the singing to induce a state of spiritual love and kinship with your angels.

62: Chant Angel Names, Prayers, and Affirmations

In the faiths of Buddhism, Hinduism, and Catholicism, chanting occupies an important place in history and practice. A seventh-century monk known as I. Tsing noted that chanting has the following several benefits:

1. Understanding the virtues of Buddha
2. Teaching language
3. Teaching poetic structure and rhythm of speech
4. Working out the lungs
5. Exercising the chest
6. Overcoming reservations about being in front of others

When the Buddhist sutras are chanted, positive forces are activated that bring blessings on humanity and the world. That is a good reason to learn to chant, but another reason is to be able to use chanting as a means of ritually preparing to meet your angels. Chanting can put you in the right frame of mind, instill feelings of sacredness, and evoke a sense of great power and peace. Gregorian chanting, named after Pope Gregory 1, the sixth-century bishop of Rome, has ancient roots, but it still has a role within Western Christian practices, especially in conjunction with ritual services and also accompanying Mass. If you enjoy hearing chants (said to be to music what calligraphy is to writing), listen to some audiotapes or CDs of chants. Whether you enjoy hearing chants of Tibetan Buddhist, Native American, Anglican, Vedic, Baha'i, or Eastern Orthodox tradition, the chanting of verses from the Qur'an, or the chazzanut (Jewish liturgical music), spend time chanting your favorite prayers or angel names. (Many Hindu chants, in fact, are based on the various names of the divine.) You can also listen to affirmations in preparation for meeting your angels.

63: Try Automatic Writing to Receive Angel Messages

If you look up the meaning of automatic writing, you'll discover that it is writing of which you have no conscious awareness of the content although you are writing it because the material comes through you from a spiritual source, or possibly from your subconscious mind. There have been numerous psychics, mediums, and New Age practitioners who profess to do automatic writing or channeling of particular archangels or ascended beings as well as those who believe they are receiving and writing messages from the spirits of deceased individuals. Some people believe automatic writing to be a way for the angels to impart divine guidance and specific messages, while others suggest that you must take care to surround yourself with the angels and the holy white light, since automatic writing can attract to you a lower-vibration entity.

The practice of automatic writing is as easy as picking up a pen and paper and inviting your angels to imprint a message into your thoughts. Give it a try and you might discover that it is the easiest way for your angels to communicate with you.

64: Write Your Worries in a Letter and Put Them in Angel Mail

Write your angel a letter. Clearly state what is worrying you or what you need, and ask for help. Then put the letter in a pretty pottery jar, decorative tin box, or a special drawer to hold angel mail. When a request is answered, find the letter containing your petition to the angels, put a gold star on the letter and file it away. Write a lovely note of thanks to the angels for alleviating your worry or pointing you to the right solution for your problem. If you are artistic, create a beautiful sacred mailbox to hold angel mail until you receive a reply (either an answer to a problem, unexpected money to resolve a financial issue, or news that you sought about someone you love and hadn't heard from in some time). Even if you are not artistic, you can purchase a pretty box from a craft store or put angel stickers on an otherwise plain box and designate it as your angel mailbox. Think of sending out your angel mail as sending a ship out on an expedition with a mission. Maybe you are waiting for your ship to come in, but how can it if you haven't sent it out?

There is something magical that happens when you have clarified what your hopes, dreams, and desires are, have taken the time to write about them, have addressed a letter to the angels asking for assistance, and are making space in your life for the manifestation of what your heart deeply desires. In a way, you are letting your angels know, in the clearest way possible, the help you need. When you send forth such a powerful request, your answer could come in some form within three days.

Part 7

SEEK HELP FROM
THE ANGELS

Have you ever experienced being late, and at your wit's end, trying to locate your missing car keys, or feeling overwhelmed when not finding a proper gift for an upcoming occasion, or even feeling frustrated when you're not able to locate a parking spot? Seek angel assistance the next time you are faced with situations that are beyond your control. You might be surprised at how easy it is to locate those keys, find the perfect gift, or suddenly find yourself in position for the best parking spot. Practicing patience when you feel like chaos reigns all around is not easy, but trusting in the power of the angels to assist you can help you learn patience; it demonstrates that you can actually make quick work out of finding what you need when you ask the angels to help. The angels ask you to trust in divine timing, and to trust that everything is happening for a reason. Being ever ready to assist you means that those divine messengers can reduce time you spend searching, shopping, and driving around in circles.

65: Ask for Angel Assistance for Fun Things (Parking Spots, the Perfect Dress, and Mechanical Repairs)

There is nothing wrong with asking for help from the angels for (what some might call) more trivial tasks, such as finding a parking place. There really are "parking angels" although you might not believe it until you discover that truth for yourself. The next time you are searching for a place to park your car in a lot or parking garage, ask the "parking angels" for a spot closest to the building entrance. Don't be surprised if the spot is open and waiting for you to pull in or if someone pulls out just as you arrive. Gamliel is one of the specific angels to call on for parking spaces and is known as the gracious gift giver.

The same strategy can be applied when you need a perfect dress for a public appearance, speaking engagement, or some other personal or professional occasion. Call on your angels to help. Tell them what style of dress you are looking for, what color, and what fabric. The more specific you are, the sooner they can guide you to the right one. It becomes fun when you realize that by asking ahead of time, you can walk into a store and go right to the dress—whittling down shopping time by enlisting help from the unseen realm.

If you find yourself stressed after discovering your garbage disposal doesn't work, the computer has crashed, or your car won't start, ask the angels to help. Request help from the archangel Michael. He is not only the great protector of heaven and earth, but he also can help you if you get lost or can't fix something mechanical.

66: Petition Angels for Protection

At one time or another, everyone has had to deal with a circumstance wherein they feel overwhelmed by a crisis, assailed by negativity, or fearful for their safety or the safety of someone they love. The following are situations in which you can call on the angels of protection:

- When visiting a hospital or someone who is ill.
- When attending a funeral.
- When you have to go to court for any reason.
- When there is a lot of negativity in your workplace.
- When dealing with authoritative figures.
- When you need to do any kind of public speaking.
- When you work as a caretaker or if you're doing any kind of healing work.
- When dealing with people who can negatively affect you in any way.

The next time one of these situations occurs, you can relax and know that help from the angels is immediate, and on its way, the minute you request divine assistance and protection. The angels will surround you in a protective bubble of light enabling you to immediately feel strong and centered. You will know beyond any doubt that you can get through any situation.

If you practice and make a conscious effort, in time you can transmute the energy of negativity, fear, and worry about safety. Instead of being affected by those things, you can choose to send love to others who might be suffering just as you are. By protecting yourself from negativity, you stay strong in your own energy; therefore you have the ability to empower yourself and everyone around you.

PROTECTION FOR YOUR CHILDREN

It's natural for parents to worry about their children, and the angels know that one of the toughest jobs here on earth is being a parent. Unfortunately, God didn't send each child with a manual, but he did send his angels to watch over and protect every one of them.

It's important to remember that when your thoughts are focused on worry and fear, your children will feel that energy even if you are hundreds of miles away. When you choose to call on the angels and you ask them to surround your children in love and protection, imagine what they would feel in comparison to worry and fear. It's in the highest and best interest for you and your children to learn how to stop and shift your thoughts from fear into faith, and the angels can help you do this.

The following are some examples of when you can invoke the angels to watch over and protect your children:

- Your child is sick and you are worried.
- You are leaving your kids with a sitter or home alone.
- Your teenager is driving or is with another teen driver.
- Your children are at school and you're concerned.
- You have older children and you're having a hard time accepting their choices.
- You have a troubled child, and you don't know what to do.
- You have grandchildren, and you worry about them.

It doesn't matter what your situation is, the angels feel your concern. From the instant that you request their assistance, they will surround you and your children in love and protection.

If you are the proud parent of a newborn, consider calling upon Laylah to protect your infant. Laylah's name derives from the Hebrew word meaning "sleep," and Laylah is an angel of the night who watches over infants and helps them transition into their physical bodies. Laylah keeps a vigil over your precious child and encircles that tiny body with an energy field of love, compassion, and protection. The following prayer can be said at any time for your newborn baby.

PRAYER TO LAYLAH

Please watch over my newborn (share his or her name). Help him (or her) adjust beautifully and easily into his new life. Let him know how dearly loved he is and that we are happy he is here and that he chose us as parents. Keep him safe and protected, and help me to feel calm and peaceful as I adjust to being a new mother (or father).

Whether you call on Laylah or another of the angels and archangels of protection, know that they are honored to assist you along your journey. They know how vulnerable you feel when fear takes over. Call them by name and know that their role is to protect you and shield you, your children, and your pets from harm.

Ask Archangel Michael to watch over your children when you worry about them or during those times when you cannot be with them. Michael will embrace them with love and safeguard them behind a protective shield. After you call Archangel Michael, notice how you feel. Trust that your children are in God's protection through the energy embrace of Archangel Michael and are being cared for in the best possible way.

Some people see their pets as their little ones and cherish them as they would cherish their own offspring. Call on Archangel Ariel for protection for your pets. Ariel's name means "lion or lioness of God." This archangel is committed to helping heal and protect Mother Nature, which includes all animals. In addition, Ariel serves as protector of the waters, watching over all bodies of water and aquatic life while also safeguarding those who ply the waters or travel upon them—for example, fisherman and sea captains and sailors. If you feel concerned about the environment and you want to do your part in protecting it, call on Ariel for support and help.

When your pets are sick ask both Archangel Ariel and Archangel Raphael to intervene. For their protection, invoke the Archangel Michael. Ask the angels to watch over your pets, and trust that they will receive the protection and healing they need.

PRAYER TO ARCHANGEL ARIEL TO PROTECT MOTHER NATURE

Archangel Ariel, I see that Mother Nature needs some healing and balance. Please watch over all of her inhabitants and see that they are protected from all harm. Please bring healing to the earth and remind me how I can play my part in helping and healing Mother Nature. Inspire me to always do more than I think I can do and to strive to leave the planet in better shape than I found it.

You can also pray to your guardian angels to safeguard pets and animals that are wild. They are also God's creations and deserving of respect. If animal policy and animal rights speak to your heart and passion, ask for angel guidance on how to help the animals you love through work involving animal policy or animal rights issues.

PRAYER TO ARCHANGEL ARIEL, ARCHANGEL MICHAEL, AND ARCHANGEL RAPHAEL FOR YOUR PETS

Archangel Ariel, Archangel Michael, and Archangel Raphael, please watch over (say your pet's name). Surround him (or her) in your healing and protective divine light. Comfort him and remind him that he is not alone and that he is deeply loved. (If your pet is sick, add the following request.) Help him to heal completely and feel healthy, whole, and vibrant once again. Thank you, Ariel, Michael, and Raphael, for safeguarding and facilitating healing of my precious animal.

Another situation that generates fear and worry is when you feel your home, the dwelling place of your family and pets, is somehow threatened or that your loved ones are not safe when they are home alone. Fear can easily set in when you're home alone and your mind wanders to that scary movie or that dreadful story from the news. Before you know it, you're in the grip of fear. What if you could feel more peace when you're home alone? What if you could trust that your children or pets were being watched over when you're not at home? Imagine how good you would feel if you knew there was someone watching over your home twenty-four hours a day while you were on vacation. Whenever you are faced with any of these situations, call on Archangel Michael and Suriel to watch over your home and ask them to keep it safe from harm. God sent you these divine helpers so you could have peace and enjoy life feeling safe wherever you are.

Denise Linn, author of *Sacred Space* and a practitioner of feng shui, says that there are house angels who serve to protect the home. She says: "I believe that the most powerful guardian for your home is an angel. Calling upon the angels to be your house guardians for protection and spiritual rejuvenation can bring a wonderful feeling of peace, harmony, and safety to your home." Use the following prayer to protect your home and property.

PRAYER FOR THE PROTECTION OF YOUR HOME AND PROPERTY

I ask that four guardian angels stand watch at each corner of my home and property. I also call on Archangel Michael and Suriel to protect my home, its possessions, and all those who stay behind. Please help everyone feel safe and at peace knowing that our home is protected in the divine white light of God and the angels. Thank you.

67: Obtain Angel Help in Finding Lost Objects

It is always maddening to lose an object such as your car keys or a piece of jewelry that you took off to wash your hands. Stop to ask yourself: Can anything truly be lost in the mind of God? God is everywhere and therefore the angels know exactly where that object is located, even if you don't. Trust that the angels will direct you to it when you ask them for their help. You can usually find it fairly quickly if you just stop your frantic searching to make the request. When you are in a hurry, your brain can become addled with emotion and numerous details, and this causes the gate to your short-term memory to slam shut. You know eventually you will remember where you left those keys or where you removed your watch and ring. But angels can quickly point you in the right direction if you just take a moment to quiet your mind and slow your breath and heart rate. In a state of calm, you can either remember the location of the lost object or find yourself walking right to it. A short prayer to the archangel Chamuel or Zerachiel can be exceedingly effective in quickly recovering lost objects. Try this one.

PRAYER FOR FINDING A LOST OBJECT

Archangel Chamuel or Zerachiel: I lost my (state the object). Please help me find it now or direct me to its location, for I believe that nothing is lost in the mind of God and you know exactly where it is. Thank you for the miracle of it being found.

During those times when you easily locate your lost object after saying that prayer, you will surely feel as though you have witnessed a miracle. Remember to say thank you when you are again on your way, after having recovered the item you misplaced.

68: Pray for Angel Guidance and Protection when Traveling

Traveling to familiar places invites joy, adventure, and excitement; however, journeying into the unknown can also generate feelings of anxiety, fear, and stress. Inviting the angels to travel with you can give you a sense of peace that you are not alone and you are being watched over, no matter what situation or complication might arise.

SEEK ANGEL ASSISTANCE FOR TRAVEL

- Request that the angels watch over the plane and the pilot, and ask that your flight be safe, smooth, and on time. Imagine angels resting on the wings of the plane.
- Ask the angels to protect your vehicle and all passengers with you; also request a clear path ahead so your travels are smooth and timely.
- Ask your angels to watch over your luggage and arrange for it to arrive at your destination when you do.
- Seek angel protection to feel safe in new locales and situations, and ask the angels to send helpful people to guide you to the best places to visit, stay, and eat.
- Solicit angel help for everything you need to make your business trip pleasurable and successful.
- Ask the angels for the perfect weather you need to get to your destination and to enjoy it while you are there.
- Seek angel protection for loved ones while you are away or traveling with them.
- Request the angels to watch over your home, your job, or business while you are traveling.
- Ask the angels to resolve travel plan glitches quickly and to provide everything you need to work through glitches with ease and grace.

See traveling as a gift. Not everyone can take time off or bear the expense of visiting loved ones far from home, experience new places just for the fun of it, or create success in a new business climate or culture. The angels want you to experience these opportunities with ease and joy. Call on them and discover how they can lighten the load and make the trip felicitous and fortuitous.

KNOW YOUR ANGELS OF TRAVELING

The following are specific angels to invoke while traveling. Simply call them by name and ask them for what you need. Know that it is an honor for them to serve you and assist you in any way they can.

- Archangel Raphael is "the patron of travelers." He watches over all those who ask for safe and uncomplicated travel.
- Archangel Michael is the protector and can keep you from harm in all situations. You can also call on Michael if you get lost and need directions.
- Suriel is the angel named in the Kabbalah who rules over earth and is considered the angel of protection. Ask Suriel to watch over your home and possessions while traveling.
- Archangels Uriel and Zapiel both work on regulating weather conditions.

Call on individual angels or invite their assistance as a team. When you assign them to their tasks notice how you feel—are you worry free, confident, and assured? You just might decide that having a team of angels assisting you with the planning and overseeing the process is the only way to travel.

69: Ask for Angel Help in Healing Your Body

The angels and archangels can assist in the healing of all types of afflictions—whether physical, emotional, mental, or spiritual. You simply have to reach out to them, ask for a healing, and trust that the process of restoring you to the perfection in which God made you has begun. Pray to the archangel Raphael whose name means "God heals" or "God has healed." Raphael is known as the "doctor" archangel who brings healing both to humans and animals. If you use your clairvoyance you might see a green emerald healing light associated with Archangel Raphael's presence. If you work as a healer, beckon this archangel to guide and assist you in your work. You might find the following prayer helpful for summoning Raphael.

PRAYER TO THE ARCHANGEL RAPHAEL FOR HEALING

Archangel Raphael, please surround me in your emerald healing light. God has bestowed upon you the power to heal. I request and accept divine healing on all levels: physical, emotional, mental, and spiritual healing. Empower me to become one with the truth. I am healed, whole, and healthy. Thank you, Raphael, for this miracle of healing.

70: Request Angel Help in Emotional and Psychological Healing

The angels support your efforts to heal by inspiring you to release toxic emotions that can permeate your life with negativity. When you feel your emotions darkening your thoughts with negativity, try breathing through the onslaught. You have to process feelings to release them. Remember this simple saying: "Feel it to heal it." Next time instead of stuffing your emotions, let yourself feel and just breathe to facilitate emotional or psychological healing. Then remind yourself to call on the angels' energy and light.

- Sit with the angels in prayer or meditation and ask them to help you heal. Share with them how you feel and explain how you want to feel.
- If you feel you need professional support and counseling, ask for angel guidance about where to seek it, whom to meet with, and when to take action.
- Ask the angels to lead you to the perfect books, classes, or support groups that can help you heal.
- Ask the angels to help you heal during sleeping and dreaming.
- Ask for a miracle and feelings of inner peace.

Allow them to guide you each step of the way, from your feelings of emotional or psychological darkness and fragmentation to light and wholeness.

If you or someone you know is suffering from an addiction of any kind, don't hesitate to pray for the intercession of the angels. Addiction can be physical, emotional, or psychological, but is always a complex disease that requires professional help as well as spiritual support and the loving understanding of family and friends. There are many types of addictions: food, drugs, alcohol, sex, and even work, for example. Addictive habits and behaviors create disharmony and destruction, not only to the addicted person but to a wider circle of family, friends, and co-workers who may feel impotent to help. If you or someone you know is suffering from an addiction of any kind, call on the angels of healing, in particular Jaoel, who works with the Archangel Michael.

Take the following steps with the angels to heal an addiction:

1. Admit and share with the angels what your addiction is.
2. Ask Archangel Zerachiel and the angels of healing for help.
3. Seek physical, emotional, mental, and spiritual healing.
4. Solicit guidance from your angels toward the people and resources you need to free yourself from addiction.
5. Take action to help yourself; ask others for help if necessary.

6. Desire healing and make a space for that in your life, meaning to change what you have to change to heal and remain healed.

Zerachiel, one of the seven archangels mentioned in the Book of Enoch, is the angel of healing who watches over and helps all those suffering from addiction. In addition, Zerachiel's duties include helping children affected by parents with addiction. A sign that Zerachiel is working with you on healing your addiction is warmth in your chest or tingling in your body. Don't hesitate to ask this powerful archangel for assistance.

71: Summon Angel Help for Loss, Grief, and Death

There are countless angel stories where the dying and their family members describe the presence of angels or a visitation from a loved one who already passed over. Those in spirit come to reassure the dying person and his or her family that no one is alone when making the transition from this world into the next.

If your loved one is about to pass over, call on Archangel Azrael whose job is to comfort humans as they die and make the transition. This powerful archangel stays with the spirit of the one who has passed on to ensure that the person adjusts to the spirit world of light and peace.

Azrael also ensures that the dying person does not suffer at the moment of death, regardless of whether or not death occurred suddenly or was the result of a long illness. This angel also provides loving support to heal grieving family members. Call on Azrael if you are grieving a loss of any kind, and ask for strength and healing as you transition through your loss.

Use the following prayer to send comfort and healing to the dying. You can also say this prayer if someone recently passed or they experienced a sudden or tragic death.

PRAYER FOR SOMEONE WHO IS DYING

Archangel Azrael and the angels of healing: Please surround (state the person's name) with your loving presence and assistance for a smooth and peaceful transition from the world of matter to the world of spirit. May God enfold him (or her) in the blanket of divine love and grant him peace.

Use the following prayer if you have experienced a loss of any kind or if you want to send prayers and comfort to others who are grieving.

PRAYER FOR STRENGTH AND PEACE AFTER SUFFERING THE LOSS OF A LOVED ONE

Archangel Azrael and blessed angels of healing of wounds of the heart: Come now, I beseech you. Provide me with comfort, strength, and peace. Help me heal the hole in my heart left by the passing of my beloved (name). Restore in me feelings of acceptance that my beloved (name) is with the angels and help me to again focus on happiness for all the blessings in my life.

Help me remember that there is an abundance of support and love available to me on earth and in the realm of spirit. As I heal and accept more love, joy, and balance into my life, help me to realize that I have the ability to affect the healing of my body, mind, and spirit when my efforts are aligned with the angels.

72: Obtain Angel Protection for Your Family and Friends

Who hasn't feared losing someone they love? Your imagination flips into overload. What started off like a small snowball worry mushrooms into an avalanche threatening your serenity. For example, your spouse is late arriving home from work, and your mind jumps to the assumption that he must have had an accident and is possibly injured or even dead. Or your child hasn't called since going to a friend's house;

it's been two hours and you fear he's in danger or has been abducted. Both are examples of negative thinking that can be shifted if you beckon your angels to assuage your fears and abolish doubt. There is no limit to the number of angels you can call on for help. Call on ten thousand angels for protection of your spouse and child, if you feel you need them. Multitudes of angels are ready to assist you at any time and in any way they can.

When fear begins to consume you, take action. Beckon the angels of protection to guard over your loved ones. Immediately ask Archangel Michael, Archangel Zaphiel, and the guardian angels to surround all those involved in a protective albeit unseen net of love and protection. Choose to have faith and imagine them being encircled by the angels' wings. See the archangels Michael and Zaphiel standing at sentry by the sides of your loved ones. Ask the angels to release your fear and replace it with peace. Remind yourself to stay present in the moment where everything is okay. Realize that your imagination has taken over and that fear is creating all the "what ifs."

Call on the angels of protection in the following situations:

- When your loved one is late in coming home.
- When a loved one is sick or not feeling well.
- When your children are home alone and you're worried.
- When your loved one is going through a challenging time and you can't be with him (or her).

- When your loved one is going through emotional issues, and you don't know what to do.
- When your loved one is traveling alone, and you're worried for his safety.

In all of these situations pray to the Divine and seek protection for yourself and those you love. Shift your thoughts from fear into faith. Ask the angels for help and know that everyone involved will benefit when you shift your intention from fear to love. Use the following prayer when you realize your thoughts are focused on fear and you need help from the angels of protection.

PRAYER FOR PROTECTION OF FAMILY
Guardian angels, Archangel Michael, and Archangel Zaphiel: Please go to my loved ones (or say their names) right now. Surround them, protect them, and keep them safe. Help me to release my fear so I can move into faith knowing that my loved ones are safe. Bless us all with peace and allow us to feel comforted and embraced in God's loving protection. Thank you.

73: Ask for Angel Assistance with Forgiveness Issues

Forgiveness means letting go of any resentment, hurt, and anger you may feel because of the actions or choices of another. Self-forgiveness means letting go of any guilt or resentment you may feel toward yourself because of the choices you've made in the past. If you really think about it, you've probably had many experiences where you've had the opportunity to practice forgiveness, both for yourself and others. Some people find it difficult to forgive and let go of the memory of a painful past experience. But an inability to forgive and release can be detrimental to your health and wellbeing. The angels of forgiveness can help you heal emotions that bind you to the past, helping you to transform your painful emotions and ultimately come to a place of forgiveness.

There is a great quote from *Healing with the Angels*, written by Doreen Virtue, PhD, "Forgiveness does not mean, 'What you did is okay to me.' It simply means, 'I am no longer willing to carry around the pain in response to your actions.'" Forgiveness releases you from the "prison" of another person's choices and actions and the effects they have on your life. You receive the following gifts when you receive the gift of forgiveness:

- Peace by letting go of old resentment and anger.
- Health when you heal painful emotions.
- Healthy relationships when you heal past ones.

- Compassion when you choose to understand why the other person may have hurt you.
- Freedom by letting go of the past and being able to move forward.
- Empowerment as you take back control of your life and its destiny.

The following angels and archangels have the specific role of helping humanity heal through forgiveness. When you ask, they give you the strength and courage to let go of painful emotions and to heal your heart. The archangel Zadkiel is the archangel who stopped Abraham from sacrificing his son Isaac. Zadkiel's name means "the righteousness of God," and he is known as the archangel of benevolence and mercy. Call on Zadkiel when you are ready to let go of judgment and guilt and heal through forgiveness and compassion. The archangel Chamuel, often referred to as "pure love in winged form," is one of the seven core archangels. Chamuel's name means "he who seeks God." When you call upon Chamuel, you may feel a loving energy around you or perhaps clairvoyantly see a diaphanous or effulgent pink color. Call on Chamuel when you need to forgive and heal your heart from any hurtful relationship, breakup, or loss of any kind. Pray to open yourself to love, not turn away from it as a result of your unfortunate experience. The powerful archangel Zaphiel is the leader of the choir of cherubim. If you have trouble with forgiving and you don't know how you can get to that point of forgiveness, call on Zaphiel to aid in resolving any problem. Zaphiel, it is said, can soften even the most hardened of hearts, so that you may experience the freedom of forgiveness. Bath Kol, mentioned in the Bible's Old Testament, is known as the angel with a "heavenly voice" and is depicted by the dove (a powerful symbol of the Holy Spirit). If you are still having a difficult time forgiving yourself or others, call upon Bath Kol and request the gift of grace so you can open your heart to heal through the power of forgiveness.

74: Seek Angel Wisdom for Robust Health and Longevity

At some time during our lives, we humans violate nature's laws. Overeating and drinking too much, excessive exercise, and sunburns, for example, can negatively impact our bodies and health. But with the right intention and commitment, it is possible to have robust health and the longest life accorded to us by our genetic makeup and God's will. What truly matters is having a good quality of life, and that means taking care of the body. If you need help with making good food choices, ask your angels to go with you to the market. Buy fresh produce and fruit, organic eggs, and as many non-packaged items as possible. When items are packaged, you not only pay for the packaging—you also pay with your health for all the preservatives, dyes, flavor enhancers and the like—that ensure the product can have an appropriately long shelf life. Consider what you eat over a lifetime and how nutrient rich the foods that you choose to put into your body are. How much, too, do you move that body? Exercise can be fun, even if it is just walking with a friend. And if you don't have a friend who can walk with you, ask your angels to accompany you. Do what you can to have robust health and longevity and seek angel wisdom to accomplish your goals. Focus on a high-quality life for as long as you live. You deserve it.

Part 8

CALL ON YOUR ANGELS FOR MANIFESTING

Look up the definition of abundance and you'll discover the following meanings: "having more than an adequate quantity or supply," "an overflowing fullness," and "great plenty." The angels will remind you that the true meaning of abundance is living in the fullness and richness of life and experiencing the abundance of life's gifts—love, joy, happiness, peace, fulfillment, and prosperity. If you feel unworthy and undeserving of having the best things in life or receiving your highest good, you will have to heal this issue or you'll block the manifesting of the good things that you want to attract. Low self-esteem and feelings of unworthiness can draw lack of abundance. You attract what your mind most often focuses upon. Abundance is your natural birthright and when you decide to accept it for yourself, you attract abundance of every kind into your life. With the help of the universal law of attraction and by asking for manifesting help from your angels, you can begin to have a life that you perhaps have only dreamed of having.

75: Summon Angel Insights for Attracting Wealth

Take the time to meditate and pray with your angels about your desires for abundance and prosperity, as the returns can be nothing short of miraculous. It is one thing to pray for your intentions but it takes on a whole new energy when you sit in meditation with the angels. You raise the vibration of your desire with focused intention and visualization. Add in the positive emotion you feel just knowing that the person, situation, or thing that you desire is on its way into your life, and you become a magnet of attraction. When you are clear about your desire, and you have the intention of attracting it for your highest good and that of others, ask for angel assistance, and take action; it is possible to attract wealth and virtually everything your heart desires.

MEDITATION FOR IMAGINING AND CREATING ABUNDANCE AND PROSPERITY

- Find a quiet place to sit, and if you choose you can put some soft music in the background. Write out your prayers to the angels. Share with them your desires for abundance and prosperity and be specific.
- Breathe in and as you exhale, release everything that transpired before you entered meditation. Breathe in

and as you exhale, imagine letting go of everything that you imagine will happen in the future.

- Breathe in and sink into relaxation, aware of the present moment where all transformation occurs.
- Summon the archangels Raziel, Gadiel, Barakiel, Gamaliel, and Pathiel, who are angels of abundance and prosperity. Ask them to create a beautiful circle of sacred light around you. Imagine them embracing you in an aura of divine love, light, and protection. Imagine within this sacred circle, the abundance of God already exists. All that you desire is already here and now in the circle. The kingdom of heaven is here on earth. Take a moment and imagine this to be true, and breathe into the abundance that surrounds you.
- Imagine you have already received what you have asked for. You are living your desires right here and right now in this sacred circle. What your heart desires has manifested. Imagine the following: What you are doing as you experience the arrival of what you desired? How do you feel? How are you enjoying your life and with whom? Imagine joy and gratitude permeating your being.
- Ask the angels to help you become one with your desires. Feel yourself in the center of this sacred circle and feel worthy and deserving of having prosperity and abundance in your life. Realize you are a magnet capable of attracting what is necessary to fulfill your desires. The angels of abundance and prosperity are

not bound by matter; in the realm of spirit and ideas they perceive your desire and can inspire you to create the right circumstances to manifest your desires. Thank them and consciously feel the energy of joy and gratitude.

- Know that God (Source) and the angels bless your desires. Your job is to trust Source and affirm that the manifestation of what you have been seeking is in process, and it's just a matter of divine timing.

- Say a prayer of thanks. Breathe in and affirm that you are open to your highest potential and your greatest good. Know that you are in the sacred circle where all your manifestations will transform from the spiritual plane into the physical plane and that you will remain in that sacred circle even after you open your eyes. When you feel ready to leave the state of meditation, simply open your eyes.

Work with the angels of abundance and prosperity and be open to the miracles that are waiting for you. They feel blessed and honored to help you, and they want to shower you with many blessings from the divine. Always remember that you are a child of God, and you deserve the best. Just ask, believe, and expect to receive.

76: Seek Angel Support for Finding Your Life's Work

When you are doing the work you were meant to do in this life, you feel upbeat, perhaps even passionate, about going to work. You are inspired by the challenges, not defeated by them, and you enjoy the problem solving. Sometimes, however, a choice you made in the past places you on the wrong career track or into a dead-end job; instead of getting up with anticipation about all the wonderful things you will accomplish doing what you love, you face each morning with dread.

You don't have to stay stuck. Do some brainstorming. Ask the angels to gather round you to inspire and support you as you map out a new career, job, or life. Start free associating and write down everything that you do in any kind of work that gives you pleasure. Once you've filled the card with pleasurable work activities, start grouping them together to see if you can see a pattern. Perhaps your life's work isn't cataloging items taken in evidence for your local police department, but rather cataloging and selling garage sale and auction items in your online store. Keep asking your angels to inspire you and point you in the right direction. Ask them to help you analyze and assess the information coming out of your subconscious through free association. Ask for meaning and insight to get back on track. Claim the life's work that will most satisfy you. Adhere to the advice of Indian sages and practitioners of yoga: Don't be attached to outcome or the fruit of your labor, but do the labor for itself in the most honorable and meaningful ways.

77: Ask for Angel Assistance to Manifest Peace in Your Life

Your home is not only your dwelling place but also the site of your sacred sanctuary. If you are like most people, you want your home to be filled with a positive, loving, and peaceful energy. When you take time to show respect, thoughtfulness, and love to family members, friends, and even to yourself, you naturally fill your home with love. The space feels energetically light and full of joy. Those who live and visit there feel comfortable and safe.

Conversely, when the home is the site of frequent arguments, criticism, and back-biting, it creates a negative environment. A dark and heavy ambience is palpable. It is not surprising that people don't enjoy being in that type of space. If you don't like the feeling you get when stepping into your house, call upon the angels of protection and ask them to clear the energy inside the home. Request that they help you understand how to generate a peaceful dwelling place and assist you in creating sanctuary.

78: Call on the Angels to Help You Find the Right Life Partner

To attract the perfect life partner, develop a clear vision about the person with whom you would like to spend the rest of your life—not just the physical attributes but the traits and qualities as well. Don't overlook other aspects that are just as important as physicality, for example, intellectual prowess, fiscal responsibility, emotional availability. Also consider important core principles like loyalty, happiness, honesty, and integrity.

The following steps will help you own your power to manifest your true desires, whether for a life partner or something equally important:

1. Picture a clear mental image of what you desire. Make a wish list and release any limited thinking or negative beliefs while making your list. Believe that anything is possible.

2. Write a positive affirmation that declares what you are claiming for yourself (such as: My perfect life partner is in the process of coming to me right now.)

3. Spend time in meditation visualizing what you truly desire. Match your visualizations with the joy and exhilaration that your life partner is en route to you now. *Have you made space in your life for him or her; are you emotionally available?

4. Call on the angels and ask them to help you manifest your desire; then surrender your wish to God and the angels.

5. Feel worthy and deserving to receive your highest good. Let go of trying to control or figure out how the manifestation will take place. Just trust that it will.

These steps are very powerful. You initiate a powerful energy by aligning your thoughts, beliefs, feelings, and visions to a desired outcome. This energy becomes the law of attraction, which draws to your reality the manifestation of the person, circumstance, or thing that you have requested. Focus time and mental energy on what you want. You will draw it to you because the law of attraction is always working.

79: Summon Angels to Tread a Fearful Path with You

The road of life is often bumpy and sometimes dark and scary. If there are places that create fear in you, but you are obliged to walk through that place of fear, summon the angels to walk with you. For example, your fear is public speaking, but your boss has insisted that you give a talk. Call your angels and tell them about your fear (also your desire to be the best you can be in that situation), and ask for their help. Prepare for the talk. Practice the talk. Believe that it will go well since you won't be alone (your unseen support group of divine messengers will be there with you). Let go of the worry about the circumstances of the talk, your delivery, and everything else associated with it. Release all your concerns to the angels. Do pay attention, listen to your divine guidance, and take inspired action when it feels right. Expect the best and accept the miracle as it unfolds. What was once a thought and a feeling will become your reality.

80: Pay Attention to Angel Numbers and Sequencing

Angels are adept at using many devices to get your attention including the use of numbers and number sequences. If you are like many people, you have a favorite number. Your angels know that what your favorite number is. If you suddenly notice it displayed on a license plate, packing slip, and building or billboard, pay attention. There are two specific angelic numbers to notice in particular because they symbolize the angels are around you—11:11 and 444. When you see these numbers on a clock, in a phone number, or even on a check, you can feel assured that you are surrounded by angel love and protection. The following number sequences and their meanings as they relate to the angels are taken from *Angel Numbers* by Doreen Virtue, PhD and Lynnette Brown.

ANGEL NUMBERS AND MEANINGS

- 111: "An energetic gateway has opened for you, rapidly manifesting your thoughts into reality. Choose your thoughts wisely at this time, ensuring that they match your desires. Don't put any energy into thinking about fears at all, lest you manifest them."

- 222: "Have faith, everything's going to be all right. Don't worry about anything as this situation is resolving itself beautifully for everyone involved."

- 333: "You're with the ascended masters, and they're working with you day and night—on many levels. They love, guide, and protect you in all ways."

- 444: "Thousands of angels surround you at this moment, loving and supporting you. You have a strong and clear connection with the angelic realm, and are an earth angel yourself. You have nothing to fear—all is well."

- 555: "Major changes and significant transformations are here for you. You have an opportunity to break out of the chrysalis and uncover the amazing life you truly desire."

- 666: "It's time to focus on Spirit to balance and heal your life. Tell heaven about any fears you have concerning material supply. Be open to receiving help and love from both humans and the angels."

- 777: "Congratulations! You've listened well to your divine guidance and have put that wisdom into fruitful action. You're now reaping the rewards. Your success is inspiring and helping others, so please keep up the good work."

- 888: "The universe is abundant and generous, and you have learned how to step into the shower of its ever-present flow. Great financial success is yours, now and in the future."
- 999: "Get to work, Lightworker! The world needs your divine life purpose right now. Fully embark upon your sacred mission without delay or hesitation."

From this moment forward be conscious of the numbers that you suddenly notice. They could be a sign from your angels trying to get your attention, or maybe they just want to send their love and reassure you that you are not alone.

81: Ask for the Highest and Best Benefits for All

There's a saying that what blesses one, blesses all. Think of this as you begin to work with your angels for your highest good. When you are joyful and excited about this great gift of life, pray and seek blessings of goodness and abundance for others. It creates good karma and also causes a ripple effect—that is, your exuberance about life and your joy in living it ripples outward to touch others. As goodness begins to unfold in your life through the help of your angels and the law of attraction, you can choose to use some of your time to help others. Perhaps you could volunteer to improve the quality of life for another; or you might work in silence, praying, meditating, and working in the spiritual spheres for another person's highest good.

Call on the archangel Jeremiel, whose name means "mercy of God." In Judaism, Jeremiel is known as one of the seven core archangels—a visionary and available to help you turn your dreams into reality. Jeremiel will inspire you to reach for your highest goals, hold the vision of your desire until it comes true, and assist you as you create harmony in all aspects of your life. Hold love and the concern for the welfare of others in your heart. Then, calling upon Jeremiel, seek the highest good for yourself, but do not forget to ask for blessings for others.

82: Cultivate Faith and Trust in the Divine

If you want your best life now, you may have to do a frank self-examination to see what isn't working and why. What can you do differently to shift from the status quo to create a dynamic new paradigm of success and happiness? Can you learn to trust enough in God and yourself as co-creator to manifest the success you seek? The more optimism you have that things will work (because you have enlisted the Divine and the Heavenly Host to help you), the more you will attract what you desire. Optimism, faith, and trust bring you more of what you hope will manifest, and more of the goodness you desire and anticipate; doubt, disbelief, and distrust, conversely, return more darkness and despair. You are a child of the divine. The world and everything in creation is truly yours, so claim it. Believe that you are a spark of that Great Light that existed even before the dawn of creation. The Sufi poet and mystic Rumi wrote that people traverse back and forth "across the doorsill where the two worlds touch," but because they desire sleep more than discovering the secrets that the dawn holds, they go back to sleep, forgetting to ask for what they really want. Take Rumi's admonition not to sleep into your heart. Meditate at dawn, ask for what you want, and cultivate faith and trust in God.

83: Take Action and Expect Miracles

The last powerful step to manifesting with the help of the angels is to create an action list. You have no doubt heard the sayings, "As you think, so you become," and also, "God helps those who help themselves." The former addresses the need to think of yourself in positive ways and to feel ready to accept into your life what you deeply desire. If you want success but never work through the fear of having success, you won't be able to envision yourself as successful. You won't make the space in your life to have success. You won't dream it, seek it, affirm it, meditate on it, feel it, or even ask for it. Therefore, you certainly won't expect it, and success probably won't show up. However, the opposite is also true. When you can desire it so deeply that you think, feel, and do everything possible to attract success, you can expect a miracle. It won't fail to show up. Create an action list for your desire. Ask the angels to lead you in the right direction and to the right people who will motivate and inspire you. Further, ask the angels to instill in your thoughts ideas for creating the necessary conditions so that your deepest desire can manifest. Work as if every action you perform creates a powerful magnetic pull for that desire to show up. Believe in it. Expect it. The Polish Jewish-American writer and Nobel Laureate Isaac Bashevis Singer wrote, "For those willing to make an effort, great miracles and wonderful treasures are in store."

Part 9

ENLIST ANGEL HELP FOR EVERYDAY LIFE CONCERNS

Small blessings and significant miracles happen every day in your life whether or not you are conscious of them and whether or not you consider them to be ordinary events or blessings. You awoke to behold a new day. Perhaps you hadn't noticed that the dogwood broke into flower or that the mourning doves started a new family in their nest under the porch eaves. Maybe the child in your neighbor's yard took his first steps out of his mother's arms, or the old woman across the street buried her nose in a newly bloomed rose. Did you see those events as miraculous or ordinary? Do you see that, following your awakening, there is the promise in each moment of your day to do something awesome, to make a difference in your life or in the lives of others, to effect a change in the world—or just your world. Each of the afore-mentioned events is nothing short of miraculous. To view them through that lens, you may have to shift your percep-tion. *A Course in Miracles* states, "Miracles should inspire gratitude, not awe. You should thank God for what you really are. The children of God are holy and the miracle honors their holiness, which can be hidden but never lost." To witness or experience miracles in your life, be willing to accept or initiate the following:

- Understand you are a child of God and you were created in the likeness of God. Only your sense of duality creates the sense of separateness. The divine light shines within you.
- Open your heart and your mind, and believe that everyday miracles of seemingly ordinary events really do happen.
- Imagine that all that you desire and seek for your everyday life concerns is already here in the present moment.
- Know that you are worthy and deserving of receiving miracles, no matter how mundane you think your desire or need is.
- Visualize or imagine the miracles you desire.
- Believe and have faith in yourself, God, and the angels.
- Expect and allow the miracles to appear.

The next time you awaken, consider saying a prayer of thanks for the gift of a new day or another chance to live differently, seeing the world anew through the lens of miracles and blessings.

84: Know the Extraordinary Exists Alongside the Ordinary

In literature and art, there is a genre known as magical realism. In essence, in art it is an aesthetic style in which fantastic or dreamlike elements combine with realism. The genre as an art style began in the years following the First World War. Writer Franz Roh coined the term "magical realism" in 1925 when referring to art that held within its subject a mystery or secret. In other words, in the subject matter of a painting or novel, ordinary elements would be present, but there would also exist the extraordinary—fantastical or magical aspects. Andrew Wyeth's painting, *Christina's World,* and the novels of Gabriel Garcia Marquez characterize works of magical realism. In the former, you see a young lass, perhaps a schoolgirl, looking at a distant farm from where she sits in a field. On closer examination, the girl isn't a girl at all but Christina Olsen, a disabled woman in her fifties with thin, deformed arms who is dragging herself toward her rural farmhouse. As the viewer, you may think you know what you are seeing; however, magical realism illustrates that magic and mystery and phenomena, that you may not immediately decipher correctly, can hide in plain sight.

Life works that way too. The angels can help you dig deeper to better understand the magic in life that is just below the surface. You may not understand how it works or exactly when it will work, but you can trust that it is there. In times of need or desire, you can call upon that invisible angel network, summoning its power and energy to work miracles in your ordinary everyday life.

85: Practice Patience and Trust in Angelic Aid

The Russian writer Leo Nikolaevich Tolstoy said that the two great warriors are patience and time. Cultivate both to witness the powerful and miraculous manifestation of your dreams. Develop trust in the aid of your angels and the grace of God with whom you co-create. Patience involves waiting, but not necessarily passive waiting. Great power comes from giving up power, and your ego doesn't have to concern itself with every detail to bring about fulfillment. So while you wait, align your will with divine will. Know the aid you have requested is en route. Start working on the items on your to-do list. Do your affirmations and visualizations. Beckon the angels and trust that they are already working on the other side of the curtain between the worlds of spirit and matter. There need be no struggle. You simply become more powerful because the more you practice patience and gain an intimacy with God and the angels, the more you are yoking your will and intention with the power of the divine.

If you are someone who needs instant gratification, you may need to work harder on practicing patience. In ordinary life, many people are skeptic about miracles, psychic phenomena, miraculous and synchronous events, and holy apparitions. They doubt instead of considering the possibility that there are different energy levels, states of consciousness, and shifting energy patterns at work—all within the space-time continuum we think of as our universe. Much remains unknown about the world of matter, and perhaps even less is known about the world of spirit. Things can and do unfold without your ego dictating every detail.

EXERCISE TO PRACTICE PATIENCE

Think of something currently going on in your life that requires patience. With your journal or paper and pen in hand, ask your angels to surround you. Breathe in and out while imagining it is their energy of love that you breathe. Write the question, "Dearest angels, is there anything I can do today that will bring me more peace?" Listen, feel, and allow the answer to come. When you finish, ask the angels if there are any action steps you can take. If the angels share with you that you need to be patient, and they advise you to accept what is right now, pray for patience and surrender the issue to the angels for divine resolution. Know that you have the power to choose peace in any moment. Simply affirm, "I am patient and the angels will show me what I need to know."

86: Release Negative Feelings of Guilt, Anger, and Resentment

As you have already learned, negative feelings beget more negativity in your life. If you have a mostly negative outlook on life, usually seeing the cup half empty rather than half full, find one thing about which you can feel hopeful and positive. Seek ways to release feelings of anger, guilt, resentment, hostility, jealousy, and self-pity. It may not be easy since negative emotions can get a strong hold on your thoughts. That is why some people use yoga to imagine emotionally "letting go" while others seek help from a support group to stay upbeat, optimistic, and hopeful. Talk to a clergy member. Ask for help from the angelic realm. Seek professional counseling if necessary. Surround yourself with positive people. Join your local Optimist Club.

Remember that your thoughts create your experiences and your reality. When your thoughts are positive you create happiness, joy, fulfillment, and peace. If your thoughts are focused on the negative, you see your life through that lens, and that can produce fear, sickness, and stress. This is why it's so important to stay conscious of your thoughts. Strive to be aware of how and when a negative thought intrudes (awareness), take note of triggers in your body or environment, and calmly redirect the negative thoughts by replacing them with positive messages that are constructive and encouraging. Break out of habitual routines that keep you stuck. If you change nothing, nothing will change. So try bringing about a shift in your thoughts, words, and deeds. Send out a call to your angels, and you'll soon see how life not only feels different, but how it *is* different because you are viewing it through a different lens.

87: Ask the Angels for Help in Releasing Worry

What worries you? How much time do you spend worrying about things that are out of your control? Do you ever look back and realize how much time and energy you spent on wasted worry? Do you worry and fret over things that seldom, if ever, happen? Worrying can mentally exhaust you and has even been attributed to illness.

Some worries are justified and can help you make better choices. For example, the doctor says you're overweight, and because you worry you choose to eat better and exercise. There are the worries that cause needless stress such as worrying about what other people think, or obsessing during the day about whether you locked the door when you left the house, or even worrying about the safety of your teenager, who is driving in the snow. When it comes to worry, the angels can help you. Your job is to recognize your worry and then choose to release it to the angels.

Follow these steps to release your worry, and ask for help from the angels:

1. Recognize and acknowledge your worry. Spend a couple of days being conscious and record all the things you worry about—both your minor and major worries.

2. Sit with your list and ask yourself, "How does it make me feel to worry about these things?"

3. Examine your list again and ask yourself, "How many of those things I feared or worried about actually happened?"

4. Take responsibility. Is there anything on your list that you are worried about that's within your control and you can affect? If so, list your action steps.

5. Surrender the rest of your worries to the angels. Let go and let God find the divine resolution to all your concerns.

The angels will encourage you to raise your vibration from negative thinking to positive thinking. Free your mind, body, and spirit from worry and feel empowered to live life more fully, joyfully, and in tune with Spirit.

88: Seek Angel Help for Dealing with Concerns Involving Children

Many issues confront parents today that involve the safety, happiness, development, growth, and wellbeing of their children. Each age group of children faces special challenges that evoke parental concerns, and legitimately so. Newborns and toddlers often remain under the watchful eye of their parents, but after a child reaches school age, children become the responsibility (during the school day) of teachers and school staff. Adolescents, tweens, and teens all need parental love and support to properly develop and feel safe even as they are pushing the boundaries of home and the world (their developmental task). Whatever challenges you face or concerns you hold involving your children, do what you can; but also remember that you can call on your angels and theirs for support, love, and protection.

God assigned your children at least two guardian angels to watch over them for their entire lifetime. Whenever you need help with your children, summon and talk to their guardian angels. Tell them your worries and fears, and ask them to help your child. The hard part may be simply letting go, and trusting the angels to do their job. Be open to the miracles of their assistance. Remember that in God's kingdom, there are countless numbers of angels to serve humanity. When you feel the need, you can assign hundreds or thousands of angels to safeguard your children. Imagine the peace of mind you will have. Isn't it worth taking the time to invoke angel assistance?

89: Pass Messages to Your Children's or Spouse's Guardian Angels

You can pass messages to your children and spouse through their guardian angels; or you can simply call out to their angels to ask for assistance for your family members. Whisper, say, or mentally pray something such as, "Beloved guardian angels of (insert name of your son, daughter, or spouse)," and then state your need. If your concerns are centered upon your spouse's emotional, physical, financial, legal, or other issues, call upon his or her guardian angels for aid. That empowers you to be helpful and also brings you peace of mind.

When the assistance you seek is because of a crisis or acute injury or illness, remain calm. Ask your own guardian angels to give you strength and clarity of mind, but remember that you can also beckon the angels of the person for whom you are most concerned (the one in crisis or who has suffered an illness or injury, for example) and ask that person's guardian angels to render help and comfort.

90: Practice Acceptance and Find Peace in Each Moment

Peace is a feeling you experience when you are calm in mind, body, and spirit. Choosing your thoughts carefully is a step toward peace, but making choices and taking action to create more peace in your life is equally important. When you are in crisis mode, it is virtually impossible to feel peaceful because of the powerful "fight or flight" hormones that have flooded your brain. But when there is no crisis (or it has ended), and you realize that there is still pain, sadness, or stress in your life, take a step back and reflect. Ask yourself, "What do I really want, and what will bring me peace?" Peace can require acceptance of what you cannot change, or it can require change that can cause you to fear or worry. Call on the angels for courage, and ask them to support and guide you as you become more accepting or make the necessary changes to move forward. You deserve serenity, and it's your divine right to have peace. Mohandas K. Gandhi, the great Indian leader counseled, "Each one has to find his peace from within. And peace to be real must be unaffected by outside circumstances."

Peace is calm, quiet, tranquility, harmony, stillness, and serenity. Just as you can choose to have drama and chaos in your life, so you can also choose at any moment to experience peace. It doesn't matter where you are, whom you are with, or what's going on, you can always elect to direct your thoughts toward peace. As you take breaths in and out in several cycles, mentally ask the angels to encircle you so you may feel tranquility. Affirm, "I choose peace. I am peaceful." Believe that you can have peace.

PRAYER FOR PEACE

Dearest angels, I call on you now to help me find peace (share with your angels the situation that is disturbing your peace). I realize peace is found in the moment so please help me stay present to this moment, knowing that I am okay right here and right now (breathe with the angels). Help me to become one with peace in my mind, body and spirit. I surrender this situation to divine intervention and I trust that all is well. Thank you, angels, for this gift of peace and for your continued love and support.

91: Use Prayer to Make Requests and Give Thanks

A passage of a tranquility prayer states, "God grant me the serenity to accept the things I cannot change; the courage to change the things I can; and the wisdom to know the difference." The assistance being sought from God is sublime. When you put the serenity prayer into practice, you open a pathway to peace. As the prayer proclaims, serenity comes when you can accept the things you cannot change. Have you ever tried to change someone, expecting them to be different or wanting them to be someone you thought they should be? You feel exhausted and disappointed in the futility of your effort while they may feel frustrated at not "measuring up" or think that you don't care who they really are. Peace comes when you finally accept that person for who he or she is. If your relationship with him or her still works, great; if not, find the courage to make your own choices or go your own way.

It's the same for situations in your life. You need to ask yourself, "Is this something I can change, or is it out of my control, and do I need to accept what is with peace?" For example, the price of gasoline goes up, and you decide that you can't control the price of gasoline, but you can conserve gas and plan your errands accordingly. You can find peace in accepting what is (the price of gasoline), and you can also feel empowered to make choices that will benefit you (conserving gasoline); in the end you create peace.

THE SERENITY PRAYER

God, give us the grace to accept with serenity the things that cannot be changed, the courage to change the things which should be changed, and the wisdom to distinguish the one from the other.

It takes patience and determination to accept the things you cannot change. Call upon God and the angels, and ask for the healing that you need in order to let go. If the words from the serenity prayer have meaning to you, use the prayer. Permit yourself to be blessed by its words of wisdom. Use prayer, too, to give thanks and appreciation for the blessings that flow to you in every minute of every hour of every day. When you feel down, depressed, or sad, list those blessings that you count on each day but may forget to thank the Creator for—examples might include being able to walk, talk, breathe, see, taste, feel, love, think, and so forth.

92: Address Prayers to Specific Angels

Although it is easy to call out to the angels or your guardian angels, it may be more meaningful to you to address specific prayers to specific angels. The archangel Jeremiel is considered the angel of visions, so feel free to share your grand dreams for your life with Jeremiel. Archangel Raziel, whose name means "secret of God," is believed to be the knower of all the secrets of the universe and its workings. Raziel is akin to a divine wizard and can teach you about manifestation and working with the power of divine magic. Archangel Uriel is also known as the "fire of God," and notable for his gift of prophecy. Suriel is an angel of healing and also an angel of death, with the power to manifest anything from nothing. Suriel can assist you in living your wildest dreams on Earth and also to experience heaven.

Read about Uriel in the Book of Enoch, an apocryphal text (not found in the Old Testament, but relative to it) that declares Uriel as "one of the holy angels, who is over the world . . . the leader of them all." It was Uriel whom God sent to warn Noah of the Great Flood. If you want to learn about alchemy and the power of manifestation, call on Uriel to teach or reinforce your belief in the power of divine magic and alchemy.

As you can see, you have not just one angel but an entire team who can help you manifest your specific desires. With their assistance, you can embrace the idea that anything is possible, and the miraculous can be part of ordinary everyday living. Take time to pray and meditate with them. Invite them into your life. Invoke them in times of need. Through their help and guidance, you can experience the magic of the divine.

Part 10

FINE-TUNE BODY, MIND, AND SPIRIT TO STRENGTHEN ANGEL COMMUNICATION

Most of us use our senses to detect things in the world of materiality and matter, but what about sensing things at the quantum level of particles of energy, and where light is born, or levels even higher? Sages, adepts, and mystics have knowledge of such places. Deepak Chopra, physician and author, calls such mystics "quantum navigators," noting that they understand that all that we detect in our physical world had to begin in the mind of God as thought. Mystics cross the invisible zones between the worlds of matter and spirit to journey closer to the mind of God. Some have described such a high, holy realm as being where energy is like light, and streams through oneself. Additionally, there you sense a lightness of being (even floating or feeling weightless). Sensory perception (touch, feel, taste, sight, scent, and sound, for example) is heightened, and breathing and heart rates slow as a sense of timelessness. What the late Madeleine L'Engle (*Walking on Water: Reflections on Faith and Art*) called "flow" sets in.

The way to consciously embark upon that journey is to refine your senses, strengthen your mind to be able to focus and hold awareness on a particular point for some time, and elevate your energy vibration. You have many options for achieving increased sensitivity of your senses and ever-higher states of consciousness. Start with techniques that heighten and expand awareness since awareness will be an important tool for detection of the angels.

93: Clear Mental and Emotional Blockages

When you are stuck and you don't know how to move past the place you are in, you have a block that needs releasing. If you feel a sense of urgency to remove yourself from a relationship or circumstance in life, you need to release the blockage. If you feel dread or fear about something, you need to release whatever is causing those feelings. We all get stuck at certain times in our lives. But the good news is that there are many easy ways to get unstuck, unblocked, and moving again. Try the following to effect change:

- Resolve that you want to examine the problem, release the blockage, and move on.
- Imagine how it would feel to be past the releasing stage.
- Brainstorm ways to release your blockage. (Draw a wheel with ten spokes, and put one idea at the end of each spoke.)
- Choose one or more of your brainstormed ideas to execute.
- Take action to release the blockage.
- Don't let the problem back into your life or mind.
- Repeat the steps if necessary.

If you do nothing, you risk staying stuck or blocked. But do one thing differently, and you shift the status quo. It's that easy. Once you've removed your blockage, focus on learning meditation or deepening your concentration and awareness of the details of your daily routine. This is so you'll notice when the angels draw near; you'll sense something is different. You have to boldly go into the direction of the angels, ascended masters, and God. There are many monikers for God, including Infinite Intelligence and Divine Mind. Use your mind to help you decipher the world of spirit, and to draw near to that world, perceive it with clarity using intuition to penetrate through from the material world through the quantum to the virtual; there you will experience what mystics have—the numinous presence of the divine and the angels.

94: Try Alternative Healing Modalities to Fine-Tune Body and Spirit

Integrative medicine focuses on treating the whole person, not just the parts of their bodies affected by illness. This relatively new approach to treatment combines alternative healing modalities such as acupuncture, massage, biofeedback, yoga, tai chi, breathwork, and other stress-reduction techniques to complement traditional or mainstream medical treatments. Drawing upon modalities (some ancient) used in other cultures, integrative medicine stresses the importance of seeing the person as whole and not the sum of his or her diseases.

You can use one or many of these healing modalities including nutritional counseling, biofeedback, and chiropractic treatments if they make you feel better and help you toward achieving a healthy wholeness that is more conductive to spiritual practice. You will have a difficult time meditating or practicing yoga postures if your sciatica is screaming with pain. Treat the body and get the healing you need (ask the angels to guide you to the right modality and clinic or doctor). Maybe you just need the human touch because you have been grieving. If that's the case, getting a massage on a regular basis could prove efficacious.

95: Practice Chakra Clearing

In art, chakras or energy centers are often depicted as flowers, with varying numbers of petals or wheels of energy with spokes. Although in some spiritual traditions the numbers of the chakras and their positions may vary, it is generally accepted that there are basically seven chakras, and each serves as a nexus or point of energy to vitalize the human body. Carrying the energy are *nadis*, similar to nerves. This vast network of *nadis* empties into the chakras that sit along a central channel. The central channel, the *sushumna*, has two smaller channels on either side (the *ida* and the *pingala*); all three align along the spinal column. For centuries, Indian yogis have worked with these *nadis*, channels, and chakras to clear blockages and awaken the latent *kundalini*, the divine energy that bestows union with God when it rises through the chakras and pierces the *sahasrara* or crown chakra. As the *kundalini* rises, each chakra's special powers are activated. For example, you may become clairsentient or clairvoyant. Sometimes a seeker of truth experiences a spontaneous awakening of that divine energy, but more often awakening is the result of actions taken by the seeker with the help of a yoga master or teacher.

To clear blockages and rebalance the chakra energies, do yoga poses, *pranayamas* (various breathing techniques, as previously explained), repetitive movements such as circular movements of the head or body (like spinning), visualizations (to release negativity that you might be holding onto), and intoning of certain sounds that correspond with each of the chakras. There are many helpful books available in the market today explaining how to work with the chakras. Other modalities might involve *reiki* and hands-on healing, chanting of mantras, aromatherapy, and sound, color, or light therapies.

96: Nurture Your Intuition and Develop Psychic Powers

In your ongoing effort to fine-tune your body, mind, and spirit through healthy practices, you will naturally become more attuned to the world of spirit. Take a class or work with a teacher to develop your intuition and psychic powers.

These are God-given gifts. Everyone has these latent powers to some degree. You can choose to nurture them in order to improve communication with the angels. Try the following prayer if you need a little extra help to start developing clear communication with God and the angels.

PRAYER FOR CLEAR COMMUNICATION

Dear God and the angels, I have a profound desire to feel a deeper connection with you. Please help me to clear the pathways of communication so I may easily receive your loving messages of divine guidance. My desire is to hear clearly, see clearly, and feel clearly. Help me to understand and have a clear knowing of what the messages mean. Thank you for all your help as I journey toward a deeper connection with the divine.

Another technique for nurturing your intuition so that you might be able to more easily recognize the holy presence of the angels is to concentrate on the heart chakra. As you dive deeply into meditation in the temple of your own heart, you can perceive continuous sounds, including "AUM," tinkling bells, and knocking. This "AUM," however, is the supreme sound. (It has been said that "AUM" is both energy and consciousness.) It is the subtle energy vibration that underlies all of creation. You can drown in the river of that sound and awaken into the consciousness of divine mind. In the *Yoga Sutra III*, verse 35, it states that "In the heart is understanding of the mind." In the New Testament, Jesus refers to the sound in the heart when he says, "Behold, I stand at the door, and knock: if any man hear my voice and open the door, I will come in to him . . . ." (Revelation 3:20). Sacred sound or the word of God occupies a preeminent place in the teachings of many great religious traditions. Angels can make their presence known through the sudden tinkling of wind chimes or knocking or other unusual and unexpected sounds.

An ancient form of yoga that deals with light and sound is known as *shabda* yoga. For thousands of years, *rishis* (Hindu sages), seers, and yoga practitioners of *shadbda* yoga have emphasized that their knowledge did not come from outside sources but rather from their intuition, psychic experiences, and experiential knowledge of the inner worlds. Shams Tabrizi, the thirteenth-century Sufi mystic (widely regarded as the teacher of the poet-mystic Rumi who stumbled through the streets of Konya, Turkey, drunk with love for the divine), declared that creation came into being from sound or word. The New Testament, Saint John's gospel, opens with, "In the beginning was the Word, and the Word was with God, and the Word was God."

Go into your heart and listen. Follow the sound. It is a path to God. It will lead you into the presence of the divine. As Shams Tabrizi counseled, "Hark with the soul's ear to the sounds innumerable." The mystic was referring to the sounds that could not be heard with ears. Such inner sacred sounds can be heard in meditation and their meaning derived through the power of your intuition or inner divine guidance.

97: Pray to Receive Insight about Your Future

Someone once said, if you want to know your future, examine your thoughts now. For what you think about most is what comes to you. If you have reached a proverbial fork in the road of life and are unsure about which path to take, consider praying over it. Say your prayer at bedtime and then incubate a dream. Ask God to send the angels with a dream message. Pay attention to the symbolism in the content of your dream upon awakening, as symbols are the language of the dreaming mind. Try meditating on the "AUM" sound and then with attention at the third eye, pray to God for insight, guidance, a yes/no response, or for a sign that you cannot misinterpret.

You might also pray to God to ask for a vision about your future. Visions were common among ancient Semitic people of the Middle East who prayed to Yahweh. Both the Old Testament prophets and the New Testament apostles had visions that warned, guided, revealed, and served to strengthen faith in God. Moses was a visionary prophet, and so was Elijah the Tishbite. Isaiah had many visions and visitations from angels. Saint John the Divine, an apostle of Jesus, wrote visions about the future (especially the end times) in the Book of

Revelation, the last book of the New Testament. If you want the truth about your future from the highest source, go to God and ask him to reveal insights to you through a vision, perhaps carried by angelic messengers.

ANGEL READING FOR LIFE PURPOSE AND CAREER

You can use angel cards to do a specific reading in order to gain insight about career and life purpose. The cards can help you see what you may not be able to hear or understand for yourself.

Before you pick your cards, you will want to set your intention with the angels. Ask for specific guidance on what you need to know about your career or life purpose, and ask for the highest guidance to come through. If you have a specific situation you need clarity on, then pick your cards with the intention of getting an answer or clear insight into what you need to know.

Shuffle your deck of angel cards and call on the angels of career and life purpose. Ask them to give you the guidance you are seeking through the cards. Then spread them out in front of you and pick two cards. See if your answer is immediately shown by the cards chosen. If you are confused and you need more clarity, then ask the angels to clear the confusion with the next card you pick. Then choose that card. Write your cards down in your journal, or keep them out for a couple days. You will be surprised how accurate they really are as the day unfolds. Remember, the angels want you to receive the clarity you are searching for, so expect the answers to be revealed.

Your career and living your life purpose are two important aspects of living a full and prosperous life. It is your divine right as a child of God to be happy and fulfilled as you serve others and humanity. You are here on earth as a unique expression of the divine, and you have your special place in the big picture. Have the courage to discover what that place may be if you haven't already remembered it for yourself. The angels will help you in the most amazing ways if you call out and ask for help. Remember, you deserve to be in a place where you love what you do and you live abundantly and prosperously as you express your unique and special self.

98: Pray for Healing, Self-Forgiveness, and a Joyful Spirit

Prayer can be efficacious in bringing about healing. Naming your illness, whether it is in your body, mind, or spirit, can empower you to pray for its fading. It's like naming your adversary or your enemy. Perhaps you hold anger inside (psychologists say that anger turned inward can become depression), or you have hurt someone through gossip or through some thoughtless action. Seek forgiveness from the divine, but forgive yourself first. As you pray over that or any other issue or decision, ask God to open your spiritual eyes to understand the truth of your motives. Take time to consider the possible consequences of how the decisions you have made, wittingly or recklessly, will impact all areas of your life (your own mental, physical, and spiritual well being, as well as that of your family). Moreover, ask to be guided when making any decisions for your life. You want your will to align with God's will, so you can have the highest outcome of your decisions. Ultimately, we all have to live by the choices we make every day. Make choices that are divinely inspired and guided. When in doubt, always choose the high ground—what's morally and ethically right and what doesn't hurt others. Luciano de Crescenzo, the Italian writer and film director, observed that, "We are each of us angels with only one wing, and we can fly by embracing one another."

When you make good choices for your life and choose to heal old wounds (by correcting past mistakes or coming to terms with the consequences and releasing those old hurts), you begin to live more joyfully. When you choose to do work you feel passionate about, it is no longer work, but rather pleasurable activity. When you can tap the powers of your intellect and concentrate your thought energy internally, what is there than you cannot do? The impossible becomes possible. More importantly, doubts are eradicated. Tap into the invisible network of God's helpers and messengers, who are ready to come to your aid in a heartbeat. They are closer than you might think. As Saint Francis de Sales, the sixteenth century French Roman Catholic bishop of Geneva so eloquently counseled, "Make friends with the angels, who though invisible are always with you. Often invoke them, constantly praise them, and make good use of their help and assistance in all your temporal and spiritual affairs."

When you are expressing who you are and doing what you love to do from your authentic self, you are living in purpose. You share with others your gifts, your talents, and your passions. When you're in purpose, you feel good about yourself because you know you're making a contribution to help others in some way.

If you enjoy pumping gas and greeting your customers with a smile on your face, you are in purpose. If you are a nurse and you feel compassionate when assisting others along their journey from illness to wellness, you are in purpose. If you spend your day on the front porch waving to all those that pass by, you are in purpose. If you love staying home with your children and you love being a mom, you are in your purpose. Purpose is what brings you joy, happiness, peace, and fulfillment. As humans, we are meant to live our lives joyfully. That means we ought to at least try to discover our life's purpose to live with joyful spirit.

99: Try Acupuncture to Raise Your Own Vibration

Acupuncture, widely perceived as a healing tool for pain relief, provides many other benefits including the unblocking of the energy pathways in the body to restore balance, reduce anxiety, and facilitate feelings of being grounded, centered, and peaceful—feelings that are beneficial to connecting with your angels.

Borrowed from Oriental medicine (that treats the whole person—in other words, all bodily systems, not just specific symptoms or areas), acupuncture works directly with the body's *chi,* or energy. Oriental medicine holds that all bodily imbalance, diseases, and weakened states that can permit illnesses to take hold are the result of blockages of energy that flows along meridians (like nerve channels) throughout the body. As a holistic healing modality, acupuncture is used today to treat anxiety and insomnia, migraines, seasonal allergies, back pain, muscle aches and knots, sinus problems, digestive issues, weight loss, chronic fatigue, fibromyalgia, whiplash, and even infertility. However, acupuncture's greatest benefit to spirituality seekers is its effectiveness in bestowing mental clarity—through the removal of obstructions that impede the energy flow along the meridians of the body.

Since acupuncture treatments also strengthen the immune system, many people use that healing modality to prevent illness and to maintain mental, spiritual, and physical wellbeing. Some claim that acupuncture may help you to increase energy and improve your creative processes. Needles and needling techniques can vary from one therapist to another, so even if you are sensitive or frightened of needles, you have options and can discuss them with a qualified acupuncturist or health practitioner. The point is to fine-tune your body so that the subtle energy is not blocked or impeded. You want to be in optimal health in order to become ever more sensitive to the subtle energy vibration of your angels, raising your own vibration, if possible, to attune to them.

100: Use Massage to Connect with the Presence of Angels

Massage is thousands of years old, but as a healing modality, massage offers many benefits that can affect not only physical health but emotional and spiritual wellbeing. Massage therapy can increase relaxation, reduce stress, rehabilitate a sports injury, reduce anxiety and depression, and relieve pain. Massage therapists routinely use their fingers and hands to manipulate your muscles, but they may also use their elbows, arms, and feet. A great massage can shift the weight of grief and sadness, remove knots and blockages, and evoke the restorative feelings of pleasure and comfort of the kind that only human touch provides.

You will notice after receiving a massage that your body no longer holds tension. Muscle knots that can be painful or even cause referral pain elsewhere in the body are eliminated through massage. You feel wide open, unblocked, and supremely relaxed. That is the perfect state in which to invite the angels to communicate with you. As you rest in a relaxed but focused awareness, you can more easily disconnect from the senses and tune into paranormal manifestations, perhaps even in the numinous presence of the divine and the angels.

101: Cultivate Loving Lifelong Relationships with the Angels

As you grow in knowledge about angels on whom you can call for assistance for any need or desire, you will find it ever easier to cultivate loving, lifelong relationships with those powerful and beautiful spiritual beings. With their help, you will yourself become supercharged, raising your vibration to every higher frequency, empowered to manifest a joyful, fulfilling, and rich life in the here and now. In other words, you will be able to set your intentions in motion, manifesting heaven while still on Earth.

In heaven there is no time between a thought and its manifestation. When Jesus focused his thoughts on water at the wedding at Cana, the liquid instantaneously transformed into wine. This is the reality of what can happen when you align more closely with the higher heavenly forces. Things can happen at the speed of thought or even faster. When you set your intentions and you focus on your desires, you are creating your reality. The ultimate and most powerful place to be when you set your intentions is one with God, the creator of all things.

Spend some time journaling, or visualizing in meditation, what your personal heaven on earth would look and feel like.

What dreams and desires would you like to manifest in the following areas in your life?

- Relationships and family
- Body and health
- Emotional and spiritual wellbeing
- Job, career, or life purpose
- Financial
- Home
- Fun, travel, and creativity

After you are finished with your list, give it to the angels and say the following prayer.

REQUEST ADDRESSED TO THE ARCHANGELS

Archangels, I come to you sharing my dreams and desires. You, who are with God and have the power to create miracles, please help me to recognize the divinity within myself. Help me believe in the power of miracles and divine magic. Deliver to me the gifts of manifestation and empowerment so that I might be a magnet of all that is good and pure and aligned with divine will. I can draw into my life everything I need to live my life in tune with Spirit while I remain on Earth. I ask for blessings for my highest good and for the highest good of all others. In appreciation, I offer you my love and heartfelt thanks.

Appendix A

THE ARCHANGELS
AND ANGELS

ARCHANGELS

NAME	MEANING OF NAME	TYPE OF ASSISTANCE
Archangel Ariel	"lion or lioness of God"	Protecting the environment, animals, and the waters, protection if you travel by water, help with sick or lost pets, relationship harmony, divine magic, and manifestation
Archangel Azreal	"whom God heals"	Comforting the dying and grieving, transitioning from this life into the afterlife, communicating with loved ones who have passed
Archangel Chamuel	"he who seeks God"	Finding lost items, healing of the heart, compassion, relationship healing including forgiveness, finding true love, enhancing your current relationship, career, and life purpose
Archangel Gabriel	"God is my strength"	Clear communicating with God, life purpose involving the arts, adopting a child, fertility or child conception, communicating with spirit or your unborn child

ARCHANGELS

NAME	MEANING OF NAME	TYPE OF ASSISTANCE
Archangel Haniel	"glory of the grace of God"	Grace, meeting new people and creating new friendships, finding true love, discovering and enhancing your spiritual gifts, developing clairvoyance and your psychic abilities
Archangel Jehudiel	"praise of God"	Divine direction, building self-esteem and confidence, getting a career
Archangel Jeremiel	"mercy of God"	Manifesting your heart's desires, creating your best future, understanding prophetic information, understanding and interpreting your dreams, and creating life reviews to take inventory
Archangel Michael	"He who is like God"	Protecting children, protection during travel, protection of all kinds, mechanical difficulties, patron saint of policemen, releasing and shielding from negativity, chakra clearing, courage, strength, self-esteem, motivation, direction, and life purpose

ARCHANGELS

NAME	MEANING OF NAME	TYPE OF ASSISTANCE
Archangel Raphael	"God heals" or "God has healed"	Healing of all kinds, protecting animals, protecting travelers, protecting and watching over pets
Archangel Raziel	"secret of God"	Divine magic, manifestation, alchemy, abundance, prosperity, spiritual growth, enhancing psychic abilities, understanding esoteric information, and sharing the wisdom of the universe
Archangel Sariel	"light of God"	Creating loving relationships, healing and enhancing relationships, guiding through dreams, and interpreting dreams
Archangel Uriel	"God is light" or "fire of God"	Weather, prophecy, bringing light to a situation, manifestation, divine magic, and alchemy
Archangel Zadkiel	"the righteousness of God"	Healing guilt, emotional healing, releasing judgment, healing with acceptance and compassion, and helping with forgiveness for self and others

ARCHANGELS

NAME	MEANING OF NAME	TYPE OF ASSISTANCE
Archangel Zaphiel	"God's knowledge"	Protecting and watching over children, healing of the heart, forgiveness of self and others, healing anger, and weather conditions
Archangel Zerachiel	"command of God"	Finding lost items, healing addictions, and helping children affected by parents of addiction

ANGELS

NAME	MEANING OF NAME	TYPE OF ASSISTANCE
Barakiel	"God's blessing"	Good fortune, abundance, maintaining a positive outlook and encouragement
Bath Kol	"daughter of the voice"	Forgiveness of self and others and healing of the heart
Gadiel	"God is my wealth"	Releasing negativity, abundance and prosperity, finding life direction, transforming disagreements into compassion and forgiveness
Gamaliel	"recompense of God"	Miracles, experiencing more joy and happiness, gifts of all kinds, abundance and prosperity
Gazardiel	"new beginnings"	Finding a new career, getting a raise, illuminating your path ahead, and opportunities

GUARDIAN ANGELS

NAME	DESCRIPTION	TYPE OF ASSISTANCE
Hasmal	Known as "the fire-speaking angel" who guards the throne of God	Releasing limiting beliefs, discovering your divine purpose, and creating your highest potential
Laylah	"angel of the night," his name comes from the Hebrew word meaning sleep	Watching over new-born children and new mothers
Pathiel	"the opener"	Opening the gates to manifestation, abundance and prosperity, wishes and desires, and solving computer problems
Suriel	Suriel is named in the Kabbalah as the angel who rules over the earth	Protecting your home and possessions, manifesting your heart's desires, letting go of your limiting beliefs, and experiencing heaven on earth

Appendix B

GLOSSARY

Abundance
Having more than an adequate quantity or supply; an overflowing fullness and great plenty.

Affirmation
Declaring the truth through a positive statement.

Alchemy
A power or process to transforming something common into something special.

Angels
Messengers of love who serve as guardians and helpers between heaven and earth.

Angel cards
A deck of cards used for doing angel readings. The cards have various illustrations of the angels and they each have a message of divine guidance.

Angel reading
A method of divination where you connect to the angels to receive messages of divine guidance about all aspects of your life.

Angelic realm
A spiritual realm of pure love where God's divine helpers reside.

Apparition
When an angelic being or a deceased love one becomes visible and you can see them with your eyes open.

Archangels
A higher order of angels that oversee the other angels. They have the ability to be with everyone simultaneously.

Ascended Masters
God's divine helpers. These beings of light walked before you on this earth, and during their lifetimes they were great teachers. They have now ascended into heaven and their role is to help all those that need them.

Ascension
When in reference to Christ, it means the rising of his body into heaven. In New Age terms it means transforming your energy from a lower vibration into a higher vibration.

Attunement
To adjust or harmonize your vibration with the angels.

Beliefs
A mental acceptance or conviction that something is true.

Chakras
The seven spiritual-energy centers of the body.

Chanting
To recite something in a repetitive tone or to make melodic sounds with your voice.

Cherubim
The guardians of the fixed stars, keepers of the heavenly records, and bestowers of knowledge. Cherubim are in the first triad of the hierarchy.

Clairaudience
Clear hearing. This is when you experience or hear clear thoughts or words flowing through your mind, and no one is physically there talking to you.

Claircognizance
Clear knowing. When you have an inner knowing, you feel very strongly that something is true or you know beyond any doubt that you need to take action.

Clairgustance
Clear taste. When you experience this you have a clear taste of something in your mouth without any explanation of why it's happening.

Clairolfactory
Clear smell. When you use this ability, you can smell something even though it's not physically in your presence.

Clairsentience
Clear feeling. This is when you receive information as a feeling in your body.

Clairvoyance
Clear vision. This is when you have visions, images, or symbols presented to you through your inner vision rather than your eyesight.

Coincidence
When two seemingly connected things happen at the same time for no apparent reason.

Discernment
The gaining of insight or understanding about something that might have been confusing.

Divine Guidance
Receiving clarity, direction, or inspiration from a divine source.

Divine Inspiration
When you are guided or motivated by God and the angels to take action and express divine will.

Divine Intervention
When the angels intervene and perform a miracle.

Divine Magic
A magical occurrence as a result of divine intervention.

Divine Resolution
When a problem or an issue is resolved miraculously by the divine.

Dominions
Angels in the second tier of the hierarchy. They are the divine leaders who regulate the duties of the angels below them in the hierarchy. They are the angels of intuition and wisdom and the majesty of God is manifested through them.

Earthbound spirits
Deceased humans who are hanging around the earth plane. Some people refer to them as ghosts.

Ego
The part of your personality or self that sees itself as separate from God. It usually wants to be in control, and it focuses on fear.

Energy
An supply or source of seemingly unlimited power.

Faith

A firm belief in something for which there is no proof.
Another meaning is the belief and trust in God.

Guardian Angels

Your personal tutelary angels. Everyone has at least two
guardian angels who were gifted to you by God.

Guided meditation

A meditation that is guided by the voice of the facilitator.

Heaven on Earth

Having all the experiences of heaven here on earth; bliss,
unity, abundance, miracles, wholeness, joy, peace, and
unconditional love.

Hierarchy

The order of holy beings as organized in a successive ranking
of power.

Icon

A religious image or symbol that is sometimes painted on a
wooden panel.

Intention

Focusing your thoughts and feelings on what you desire to
create and experience with determination.

Intuition
The instinctual knowing you get when you listen to your inner senses.

Invocation
Asking for help or support from God and the angels.

Kabbalah
A secret doctrine of mystical teachings based on the esoteric interpretation of the Hebrew Scriptures.

Law of attraction
When your focused thoughts, feelings, and emotions are charged with energy or vibration, and it acts as a magnet that attracts into your life exactly what you're focused on.

Life purpose
When you've found a way to express yourself that feels meaningful and significant to you. It's fulfilling and you feel passionate about it.

Manifestation
A materialized form that was created from a thought or a prayer.

Meditation
To engage in reflection, prayer, or contemplation.

Medium
Someone who communicates with deceased loved ones to deliver messages of healing and love.

Miracle
An extraordinary event manifesting divine intervention into human affairs or an extremely outstanding or unusual event, thing, or accomplishment.

Nature Angels
The angels of Mother Nature; the fairies.

Near-death experience
When someone is close to death, or they are pronounced clinically dead, and they have an experience of life after death.

New Testament
The second part of the Christian Bible that includes the book of Acts and Revelation and the canonical Gospels and Epistles.

Old Testament
The first part of the Christian Bible including the books of the Jewish canon of scripture.

Powers
The angels in the second triad of the hierarchy. These angels are the defenders and protectors of the world. They keep track of human history, and they are the organizers of world religions.

Precognition
When you receive visions or information about a future event.

Principalities
The angels in the lowest tier of the hierarchy. They are the protectors of politics and religion.

Prosperity
Being successful and thriving in financial respects.

Quantum physics
A science that deals with the effects of invisible energy. It studies the fundamental nature of the universe, and it describes the universe as very different from the world we see with the naked eye.

Sacred Space
A place of retreat where you can step away from the hectic activities of your everyday life and experience peace and relaxation.

Seraphim

The highest order of God's angelic servants who sit closest to the throne of God.

Sign

A confirmation from your angels.

Spiritual toolbox

A place in your mind where you hold all your spiritual teachings.

Spirituality

Your personal and private relationship and connection with the divine.

Synchronicity

A coincidental occurrence of two or more events that have no relevance to one another, but when the occurrence takes place, it has great meaning to the person who is witnessing or experiencing it.

Third eye

The spiritual eye that receives intuitive information and spiritual visions. This energy center is located behind the forehead and between the eyes.

Thrones

The angels in the first tier of the hierarchy; they bring God's justice to earth. They create and send positive energy to the earth and all its inhabitants.

Vibration

A characteristic emanation, aura, or spirit that infuses or vitalizes someone or something, and it can be instinctively sensed or experienced.

Virtues

The angels in the second tier of the hierarchy. They are known as the "miracle angels." They are sent to earth to bestow grace and valor.

Wish list

A list of desires and intentions you would like to manifest into physical form.

Appendix C

ADDITIONAL RESOURCES

BOOKS

Berkowitz, Rita and Deborah S. Romaine. *Empowering Your Life with the Angels.* Royersford, PA: Alpha. 2004.

Foundation of Inner Peace. *A Course in Miracles.* New York: The Penguin Group, 1996.

Hicks, Esther and Jerry. *Ask and It Is Given.* Carlsbad, CA: Hay House Inc. 2004.

Grabhorn, Lynn. *Excuse Me, Your Life Is Waiting.* Charlotte, VA: Hampton Roads, 2003.

Gregg, Susan. *Encyclopedia of Angels.* Beverly MA: Fair Winds Press, 2008.

Griswold, Trudy and Mark, Barbara. *Angelspeake.* New York: Simon & Schuster, 1995.

Paolino, Karen. *The Everything® Guide to Angels.* Avon, MA: F+W Media, 2009.

Paolino, Karen. *What Would Love Do? Transform your Fears into Miracles of Love.* Abington, MA: Heaven on Earth, 2006

Stratton, Elisabeth. *Seeds of Light Healing Meditations for Body and Soul.* New York: Fireside, 1997.

Virtue, Doreen and Brown, Lynnette. *Angel Numbers.* Carlsbad, CA: Hay House Inc. 2005.

Virtue, Doreen. *Archangels & Ascended Masters.* Carlsbad, CA: Hay House Inc. 2003.

Virtue, Doreen. *Fairies 101.* Carlsbad, CA: Hay House Inc. 2007.

Virtue, Doreen. *Healing with the Angels.* Carlsbad, CA: Hay House Inc. 2006.

Virtue, Doreen. *How to Hear the Angels.* Carlsbad, CA: Hay House Inc. 2007.

ANGEL CARDS

Archangel Oracle Cards by Doreen Virtue
www.HayHouse.com

Angel Blessings by Kimberly Marooney
www.angelblessingscard.com

Angel Therapy Oracle Cards by Doreen Virtue
www.HayHouse.com

Daily Guidance from Your Angels Oracle Cards by Doreen Virtue
www.HayHouse.com

Messages from Your Angels by Doreen Virtue
www.HayHouse.com

Saints & Angels Oracle Cards by Doreen Virtue
www.HayHouse.com

Guided Meditation CDs

Angel Attunement by Karen Paolino
www.createheaven.com

Chakra Clearing by Doreen Virtue

Healing with the Angels by Doreen Virtue
www.HayHouse.com

Spark the Light by Karen Paolino
www.createheaven.com

Meditation Music

Liquid Mind CD series
www.Liquidmindmusic.com

Steven Harper's Inner Peace Music
www.innerpeacemusic.com

Personal Readings

My center, *Heaven on Earth*, is located in Massachusetts but I work with clients over the phone. When I do an angel reading I connect with the client's angel, guides, and loved ones from spirit. During a reading I can see, hear, and feel the angels and guides around you. They share their messages of divine guidance with you and they explain why they are here to help you. Possible messages of divine guidance that come through a reading relate to relationships, finances, career, physical and emotional wellbeing, and life purpose. The readings are always insightful, uplifting, and filled with divine love and healing. I also do a variety of workshops about the angels and I facilitate an *Angel Messenger Certification Program*.

If you are interested in booking a reading or a workshop, please e-mail me at *Heavenonearth444@aol.com* or visit my website at *www.createheaven.com*.

Reverend Rita Berkowitz, MS

Rita is a gifted spirit artist and medium. She can see, draw, and communicate with those who have passed to the higher side of life. Spirit guides working with Rita's artistic talent, allow her to draw a portrait of a spirit guide or spirit loved-one that is around you. Her gifts will also allow the spirit communicator to make known the message they have come to give. If you are interested in booking a reading with Rita, email her at *Spiritrita@aol.com* or visit her website at *www.thespiritartist.com*.

INDEX

Made in the USA
Middletown, DE
25 July 2021

44754641R00146